CONSCIOUSNESS AND SHAMANISM

SCHOLARLY ARTICLES BY PETER FRITZ WALTER

CONSCIOUSNESS AND SHAMANISM

COGNITIVE EXPERIENCES IN THE AYAHUASCA TRANCE AND THEORIES OF THEIR CAUSATION

BY PETER FRITZ WALTER

Published by Sirius-C Media Galaxy LLC

113 Barksdale Professional Center, Newark, Delaware, USA

Set in Avenir Light and Trajan Pro

Designed by Peter Fritz Walter

ISBN 978-1-516835-31-7

Publishing Categories
Psychology / Ethnopsychology

Publisher Contact Information
publisher@sirius-c-publishing.com
http://sirius-c-publishing.com

Author Contact Information
pfw@peterfritzwalter.com

About Dr. Peter Fritz Walter
http://peterfritzwalter.com

About the Author

Parallel to an international law career in Germany, Switzerland and the United States, Dr. Peter Fritz Walter (Pierre) focused upon fine art, cookery, astrology, musical performance, social sciences and humanities.

He started writing essays as an adolescent and received a high school award for creative writing and editorial work for the school magazine.

After finalizing his law diplomas, he graduated with an LL.M. in European Integration at Saarland University, Germany, in 1982, and with a Doctor of Law title from University of Geneva, Switzerland, in 1987.

He then took courses in psychology at the University of Geneva and interviewed a number of psychotherapists in Lausanne and Geneva, Switzerland. His interest was intensified through a hypnotherapy with an Ericksonian American hypnotherapist in Lausanne. This led him to the recovery and healing of his inner child.

After a second career as a corporate trainer and personal coach, Pierre retired in 2004 as a full-time writer, philosopher and consultant.

His nonfiction books emphasize a systemic, holistic, cross-cultural and interdisciplinary perspective, while his fiction works and short stories focus upon education, philosophy, perennial wisdom, and the poetic formulation of an integrative worldview.

Pierre is a German-French bilingual native speaker and writes English as his 4th language after German, Latin and French. He also reads source literature for his research works in Spanish, Italian, Portuguese, and Dutch. In addition, Pierre has notions of Thai, Khmer, Chinese, Japanese, and Vietnamese.

All of Pierre's books are hand-crafted and self-published, designed by the author. Pierre publishes via his Delaware company, Sirius-C Media Galaxy LLC, and under the imprints of IPUBLICA and SCM (Sirius-C Media).

Shamanism, perennial science traditions and modern science have been relegated to different cognitive and experiential realms; they were seemingly different topics, while in reality, they belong systemically together. The need for this book is evident in a time where an intuitive and integrative approach to life is going counter to 'authoritative' scientism, and where people begin to build awareness of their multiple fragmentations.

—PETER FRITZ WALTER

The author's profits from this book are being donated to charity.

Contents

*

INTRODUCTION

*

Since leaving high school and during my extensive law studies, I was deepening my knowledge in psychoanalysis and medical hypnosis as well as perennial sciences both from the West and the East.

My law studies and work as a legal researcher taught me that so–called scientific knowledge is often a mere formula for manipulating opinion by invoking established research or scientific authorities. This is unscientific because it means to measure the knew with the parameters of the old.

Only much later, and *inter alia* through the writings of Edward de Bono and J. Krishnamurti became I aware that this form of *reductionism* is inherent in the functioning of the brain and the way perception works.

—See, for example, Edward de Bono, The Use of Lateral Thinking (1967), The Mechanism of Mind (1969), Sur/Petition (1993), Tactics (1993), Serious Creativity (1996), as well as J. Krishnamurti, Freedom from the Known (1969) and The Ending of Time (with Dr. David Bohm), 1985.

This brought me to the conviction that *exact science* is a myth because all science is relative to the observer's own set of beliefs.

Meanwhile, my insights about science philosophy are widely confirmed by quantum physics and recent consciousness research, but when I first uttered them, more than twenty years ago, I was encountering but suspicion and estrangement.

What I learnt from this is that instead of accumulating knowledge, we should always check if new knowledge we acquire *resonates within ourselves* and thus confirms our own intuition and sense of truth. For only then it is useful and reinforces our own higher intelligence. There is no knowledge outside of this source and all knowledge is thus *individual* in the sense that not all truth is valid for all.

An example for belief hidden behind *methodological* reasoning is the meeting of Wilhelm Reich and Albert Einstein in Princeton when Reich demonstrated to Einstein that the temperature difference close to the orgone accumulator contradicts the second law of thermodynamics, the so–called *law of entropy*. Einstein, reportedly dumbfounded on first sight, handed the matter over to his assistant and Reich got to hear that *for methodological reasons* the experiment could not be reproduced under the same conditions as during the demonstration.

In other cases, when Reich showed the bion reactions in burnt sand, he was told that *air germs* were causing the living cell structure in the burnt sand molecules.

The *air germs* theory was a *methodological* trick that did exactly what the Church committee did a few centuries earlier in order to *not* see the Jupiter moons through Galileo Galilei's telescope. This is how mainstream science works, on *beliefs* that elegantly are veiled by *methodological* considerations.

Through further study over more than twenty years, I became convinced that an alternative science and life paradigm always existed, and I retraced it and developed a terminology that I called *Emonics*.

—See Peter Fritz Walter, The Energy Nature of Human Emotions and Sexual Attraction: A

Systemic Analysis of Emotional Identity in the
Process of Sexual Attraction, 2015.

I also found that our science patriarchy had
relegated it to the underground, and officially
denied it. And I also found amazing parallels
between this alternative science and life
paradigm deeply hidden within dominator
cultures, on one hand, and science and life
paradigms of tribal peoples or *scientific* native
religions, such as the *huna* religion from
Hawaii, on the other.

The present article will show that there is
no split in the *cognitive assessment of natural
healing* practiced within shamanism and by
shamans when looked at through the eyes not
of mainstream science, but using the millenary
cognitive tools of *alternative science*, and
particularly our insights into the functioning of
hypnosis.

WHAT IS AYAHUASCA?

*

Ayahuasca is a brew made in South America by local shamans so as to bring about a trance for self-discovery, healing, contacting spirits or exploring consciousness. The brew consists of two ingredients, *Banisteriopsis Caapi*, also called Ayahuasca liana, and the Chacruna shrub *(Psychotria viridis)*, a Mono Amine Oxidase (MAO) inhibitor.

> —See, for more details, Richard Evans Schultes, et al., Plants of the Gods (1992), 124 ff.

There are many other entheogens used for religious purposes, and they form an integral part of shamanism. Entheogens are plants that contain psychoactive compounds, such as DMT, and others, and that, when taken at appropriate doses, produce a consciousness-altering effect upon our psyche and perception.

While there are methods to alter consciousness without plants, modern researchers agree that from a point of view of *effectiveness* there is a large gap between those latter techniques, on one hand and the use of entheogens, on the other; in fact, entheogens are several hundreds of percent more effective than non-plant based methods. Some researchers have seriously tackled the question why this is so, and one of the most persisting on this specific point was the late Terence McKenna. In his book *The Archaic Revival (1992)*, McKenna affirms that entheogenic plants contain the very essential genetic code, the basic information about the evolution of life on earth, and that for this reason their ingestion, or at least the ingestion of the psychoactive compounds they contain, leads to an *immediate opening of consciousness*, which is of course something much broader and much more intelligent to experience than mere colorful visions.

In fact, McKenna's visionary and illuminating books would never have had such a powerful impact on the consciousness change of Western society if they only talked about some entertaining hallucinogenic visions.

Anthropologists and shamanism researchers who try to understand the unique phenomenon of shamanism and reduce the entheogenic experience to a mere social game, a distraction or a search for some kind of nirvana are deeply misled. It is therefore not surprising that most anthropologists, and especially those of them who really do not understand shamanic cultures, tend to employ expressions such as 'hallucinogens,' 'narcotic drugs,' 'narcotics' or 'psychedelics.'

Apart from the fact that these plants are *not narcotics*, because a narcotic drug, such as for example *opium*, renders somnolent but does not alter consciousness, the important thing to know is that entheogens are not understood, in shamanic cultures, as leisure drugs, 'to have a nice time seeing some visions,' but really are considered as assets of the religious and numinous experience.

That is why the only expression that comes close to the shamanic mindset is the term *entheogens*: facilitators for getting in touch with the god within. And as such they form part of the religious ritual, and not of party time. This is generally little understood in most Western countries where so-called 'drugs' are usually associated with leisure, distraction, party time and sex. Yet in native cultures the very idea to for example relate an entheogenic voyage with sex would offend every shaman if told about it.

It has been equally affirmed that entheogens, apart from their helping us to reach the inner mind, also dissolve nasty and somehow destructive habits such as alcoholism, and generally help in a process of social deconditioning. Entheogens help us to see behind the veil of the normative behavior code in any given society as they show us options of *different* behavior.

What we can thus learn from taking these plants as a sort of *social medicine* is to recognize the pattern of normative behavior we are caught in and that obstructs our creativity and self-realization.

People who are socially oppressed, racial, ethnic, religious or sexual minorities, may want to inquire into the possible dissolution of rigid behavior rules and oppressive normative standards in society. They may thus look for the ultimately most intelligent catalyzer that exists to see all the options reality offers and as a result might want to engage in a consciousness-opening voyage.

Another important observation regards mental health. It has often been wrongly stated that indigenous shamanic populations were psychotic or pre-psychotic and it comes to mind that usually pedophiles, in our society, once convicted and subjected to *psychiatric expertise*, are labeled in exactly the same way.

When we remember the times of communism in Russia or read books by Aleksandr Solzhenitsyn and others, we learn that under that totalitarian regime the same murderous psychiatry with exactly that same vocabulary had been used to eliminate intellectuals who were treated as system enemies because they defended human rights and democratic values.

The effective mechanisms to defend a given *standard behavior* paradigm are all founded not upon natural pleasure-seeking behavior but upon adaptive perversity. Hence, the necessity to look beyond the fence of behavior patterns and inquire into realms that seem apart from it but aren't.

The human soul expresses its originality always in paradoxes and sometimes in extreme behavior and the very attempt to 'classify' human behavior into rigid *standards for all* is in itself an ideology—idiotology.

The more a given society puts up general standards, the more it is alienated from life and its creative roots and the more it is subject to decay and perversion.

Shamanism is an effective guidepost for reentering the realm of nature's wisdom and true connectedness to *all–that–is*.

As far as I can see, people caught in minority groupings and the social fight involved with minority lobbying hardly ever come up with beyond-the-fence solutions such as studying shamanism and experiencing entheogens, which makes for the extreme poverty of many of those movements, not to say their ultimate system-obedient stupidity.

And this unconscious system-obedience can be seen in many a limitation that social activists impose upon themselves and that are, ultimately, still system-prone. As Krishnamurti said, repeating an old wisdom: the social revolt or bloody revolution is still within the *same frame of mind* as the society it revolts against.

The entheogenic quest is therefore an inner quest, not necessarily a defeatist approach on a social level, but certainly an important add-on to any social activism for any possible social or humanitarian cause. For it opens the mind for the difference, for what Apple, in their publicity, call *Think different* and which is a very handy formula for what I try to convey here.

The shaman is not a theorist, not a scientist and not a theologian. He is practical, a pragmatist, a solution-finder and his first rule is effectiveness. He is something like a highly effective Zen manager in his universe of natural laws, and he is a communicator. He communicates with the spirit world, the world of the ancestors and the world of the animal and plant spirits.

A shaman receives his basic education from the entheogenic plant teachers, and only at a minor degree from another, elder, shaman tutor.

Shamans around the world, asked why they knew this and that secret about healing, about certain *hidden connections*, as Fritjof Capra calls holistic knowledge, or about specific illnesses, answer they knew it directly from the plant spirits.

They tend to affirm that they themselves know very little and that they just humbly ask plant spirits every time they can't solve a problem or do not find a remedy for a certain illness. And the effectiveness of a shaman, then, is exactly to maximize the response-ability he has for all possible problems he is asked to solve. This involves curing sickness, doing counter-magic, finding the right timing for harvest and even the task to solve political questions regarding tribe relations. The shaman does that by maximizing his unique communication with the invisible world.

By the same token, shamans around the world, when asked about *reality* tend to affirm that our visible reality, the one most Westerners think was the only one, is a very minor and rather insignificant part of reality and that the *real* reality is the hidden one, the one that is unveiled during the entheogenic visionary experience.

If we refuse this bias of a *more or less* in terms of reality assessment, we can still enrich our mindset with the option that there might be *parallel realities* and that all realities, visible or invisible, or visible only through facilitating drugs or other consciousness-altering devices, are equally valid and equally important. An opening of science toward parallel universes, and an acknowledgment of a multitude of possible realities that are intersecting would be a great advance and evolution of Western science.

I shall now first report my Ayahuasca journey, and then evaluate it in a hopefully objective manner, using scientific methodology to evaluate it.

HYPOTHESIS

*

My hypothesis is that the consciousness-transforming cognitive experience subsequent to ingesting the ritual brew *Ayahuasca* is not, as it is often suggested, the direct result of plant chemistry, but of the shaman's consciousness reaching the experiencer's consciousness through the medium of plant chemistry as a thought and energy transmitter.

This view is not to be understood in a reductionist way. I do not say that all is to be *reduced* to one single root cause, but propose to consider *one more option* in our scientific investigation of paranormal phenomena.

To corroborate my hypothesis I shall report a mind-opening experience with *Ayahuasca* during a visit to a Shuar native shaman in Ecuador, back in 2004.

There are several facts and events around my Ayahuasca experience that are explainable more soundly when applying my own hypothesis instead of trying to match it with the often voiced theory that psychedelic experiences are caused, as a *linear effect*, by a plant-contained chloride named DMT.

To anticipate a little on my conclusions, my hypothesis provides a *non-linear* explanation of the psychedelic experience.

My hypothesis does not deny the existence of the chloride and its possible effects on the human psyche. But I contend that the mind-opening effects noticed by the novice after ingesting the brew are a result of the shaman's consciousness impacting upon a *passive perception matrix* that is part of the plant realm and that the shaman uses as a transmitter platform.

I repeat that I do not discuss away a possible other explanation, so much the more as I myself, after the trance began to grip on me, had the impression there was an intelligence in touch with me, an intelligence that was *alien* in a way, and that I attributed to the plant realm.

Theories of Causation

*

My point is not to invalidate any of the current hypotheses about psychedelic plant substances, but to *help finding a valid theory* that shows what it is that effectively opens, modifies or expands human consciousness during the Ayahuasca experience.

—See, for example, Mircea Eliade, Shamanism (1972), Piers Vitebsky, Shamanism (2001), Ralph Metzner (Ed.) Ayahuasca (1999), Michael Harner, Ways of the Shaman (1990), Jeremy Narby, The Cosmic Serpent (1999), Richard Evans Schultes et al, Plants of the Gods (2002), Terence McKenna, The Invisible Landscape (1994), True Hallucinations (1998), The Archaic Revival (1992), Food of the Gods (1993), Robert Forte (Ed.), Entheogens and the Future of Religion (2000), Luis Eduardo Luna & Pablo Amaringo, Ayahuasca Visions (1999), Adam Gottlieb,

Peyote and Other Psychoactive Cacti (1997),
Rick Strassman, DMT (2001).

Before I am going to give some flesh and
bones to my assumption, let me report that I
found till now at least one reference that seem
to confirm my point.

As the result of a general research on
shamanism and entheogens, and particularly
Ayahuasca, that I undertook over several
years, I must conclude that most of the
researchers seem to defend a rather
mechanistic causation theory that sees the
source of all paranormal phenomena in the
chemical plant substances. For example
Terence McKenna, under the spell of his large
knowledge on ethnopharmacology, and his
brother Dennis McKenna, an enthnobotanist,
never left a doubt in all their writings on the
subject of psychedelics that causation of
altered states of consciousness is due to

psychoactive compounds in plants called *entheogens.*

The question what exactly the role is that the shaman plays in opening greater pathways of consciousness is left open or subject to speculation. Dr. Rick Strassman, a researcher on DMT for many years, has quite the same linear idea about causation and sees plant chemistry as the activating force.

> —Dr. Rick Strassman, DMT: The Spirit Molecule (2001).

I have found so far only two researchers who express a view that really makes sense. Their research seems to corroborate my own findings.

Jeremy Narby, in his book *The Cosmic Serpent (2003)*, puts up the daring hypothesis that causation is due to biophoton emission, not plant chemistry.

He observes that initially this was a valid branch of research that however from the middle of the 1970s onward disappeared from the scientific literature. What is seen in psychedelic visions, according to Narby's research, are photons emitted by the DNA.

Narby writes in *The Cosmic Serpent (2003)*:

> Researchers working in this new field mainly consider biophoton emission as a cellular language or a form of nonsubstantial biocommunication between cells and organisms. Over the last fifteen years, they have conducted enough reproducible experiments to believe that cells use these waves to direct their own internal reactions as well as to communicate among themselves and even between organisms. For instance, photon emission provides a communication mechanism that could explain how billions of individual plankton organisms cooperate in swarms, behaving like super organisms. (Id., 127-128)

Now, succinctly speaking, what Narby wants to show is that what the shamans perceive as *spirits* are in reality biophotons emitted by the cells of the human body:

> What if these spirits were none other than the biophotons emitted by all the cells of the world and were picked up, amplified, and transmitted by shamans' quartz crystals, Gurvich's quartz screens, and the quartz containers of biophoton researchers? This would mean that spirits are beings of pure light—as has always been claimed. (Id., 129)

In fact, Narby's theory does not exclude that causation might also be due to plant chemistry, but he surely concludes that what is seen, what is perceived, is not parallel reality but the reality contained in our own DNA and the *superconscious memory surface* that is connected to it. A perhaps more convincing evidence of causation being an effect of the shaman's own superconscious powers, and not of plant chemistry, is brought forward, or at least hypothesized by the American medical anthropologist and psychologist Alberto Villoldo.

In his book *Shaman, Healer, Sage (2000)*, Dr. Villoldo introduces the third chapter entitled *The Luminous Energy Field* with an entry from his journals. Don Eduardo was one of the powerful Inca shamans Villoldo studied with for many years:

> I've found that the San Pedro potion does nothing other than make me sick. (...) I'm convinced that the altered state I'm in is created by Don Eduardo's singing. And then there is the energy that he claims enters the ceremonial space when he summons the spirits of serpent, jaguar, hummingbird, and condor. (...) What I can't explain is the fact that I'm seeing energy. It only happens when I sit next to Don Eduardo. When I go more than a few feet away from him I sense nothing. It's like he is surrounded by an electric space, where the air actually tingles. When I'm inside his space I see everything he sees. (Id., 41)

The perhaps most convincing corroboration of my hypothesis comes from theosophy and the pulpit of Charles W. Leadbeater.

If clairvoyant research is or is not considered as valid scientific research under the present reductionist science paradigm is not *my* problem. It may be a problem for those who, for reasons of psychological defense or emotional distortion, or else for reasons of professional reputation, adhere to a reductionist, limiting, exclusive or even sectarian science paradigm as an ultimate compensation for their lacking emotional stability.

From the point of view of *real* science as methodically sound, holistic, mentally sane and intelligently communicated observation of nature, clairvoyance *is* science.

In his book, *The Astral Plane (1894)*, Leadbeater very much stresses the fact that we can hardly judge a human being by their acts only; in fact, as thoughts are much more important as an influence upon the world than most of us in the West know, when we go to praise somebody for his achievements and judge him or her 'a good person,' we may be completely wrong, because that person may have exerted a ravaging influence on others and the world by their self-talk, by their way of thinking about others, and by their way of judging others harshly over years and years, in their mind.

What self-talk namely creates are *elementals* or thought forms and these thought forms are more or less permanent, and gain permanence over time and depending on the emotional energy we invest in these thoughts.

And I think it's good that Leadbeater addresses this point so clearly because most people in our culture are more or less completely ignorant about the impact of thought on the world, on others and on their own karma. Leadbeater writes:

> The fact that we are so readily able to influence the elemental kingdoms at once shows us that we have a responsibility towards them for the manner in which we use that influence; indeed, when we consider the conditions under which they exist, it is obvious that the effect produced upon them by the thoughts and desires of all intelligent creatures inhabiting the same world with them must have been calculated upon in the scheme of our system as a factor in their evolution. In spite of the consistent teaching of all the great religions, the mass of mankind is still utterly regardless of its responsibility on the thought–plane; if a man can flatter himself that his words and deeds have been harmless to others, he believes that he has done all that can be required of him, quite oblivious of the fact that he may for

years have been exercising a narrowing and debasing influence on the minds of those about him, and filling surrounding space with the unlovely creations of a sordid mind.

—Charles W. Leadbeater, Astral Plane (1894), pp. 54–55.

Now, regarding the elementals that are created through thought and intent, and the gestation that is brought about by the repeated fostering of a well-defined thought pattern, Leadbeater explains that these elementals are not autonomous in the sense that they can begin to act on their own and trigger changes; they must be pushed to do so:

But the 'elemental' must never be thought of as itself a prime mover; it is simply a latent force, which needs an external power to set it in motion. It may be noted that although all classes of the essence have the power of reflecting images from the astral light as described above, there are varieties which receive certain impressions much more readily

> than others—which have, as it were,
> favourite forms of their own into which
> upon disturbance they would naturally
> flow unless absolutely forced into some
> other, and such shapes tend to be a
> trifle less evanescent than usual. (Id.,
> 55-56)

The spirits of nature, shunned by Christian fundamentalism and reborn now in the course of the New Age movement, and the revival of the folk lore of fairies, as it was, for example, rediscovered by Dr. Evans-Wentz in his remarkable study *The Fairy Faith in Celtic Countries (1911)*, and observed by clairvoyant Dora van Gelder in her book *The Real World of Fairies (1999)* have certain well-defined characteristics and they are quite distinct of human beings. Leadbeater explains:

> We might almost look upon the
> nature-spirits as a kind of astral
> humanity, but for the fact that none of
> them—not even the highest—possess a
> permanent reincarnating individuality.
> Apparently therefore, one point in which
> their line of evolution differs from ours is

that a much greater proportion of intelligence is developed before permanent individualization takes place; but of the stages through which they have passed, and those through which they have yet to pass, we can know little. The life-periods of the different subdivisions vary greatly, some being quite short, others much longer than our human lifetime. We stand so entirely outside such a life as theirs that it is impossible for us to understand much about its conditions; but it appears on the whole to be a simple, joyous, irresponsible kind of existence, much such as a party of happy children might lead among exceptionally favourable physical surroundings. Though tricky and mischievous, they are rarely malicious unless provoked by some unwarrantable intrusion or annoyance; but as a body they also partake to some extent of the universal feeling of distrust for man, and they generally seem inclined to resent somewhat the first appearances of a neophyte on the astral plane, so that he usually makes their freaks, they soon accept him as a necessary evil and take no further notice of him, while some among them may even after a time become friendly and manifest pleasure on meeting him. (Id., 61)

What this means is that by impacting upon reality through thought and intent, and through emotional focus, we actually create *elementals*, which are thought forms that are somehow embodied and individualized.

Now, what I conclude from this insight, extrapolating the research of clairvoyant Charles W. Leadbeater to shamanism, is that the shaman, when concocting the traditional Ayahuasca brew, and when focusing on it, actually builds *elementals* by his strong intent and the thought forms resulting from this focus.

These elementals then, are absorbed by the plant matrix, or the psychoactive compounds in entheogenic plants, and are transmitted to the adept who desires to be initiated by the shaman, through ingesting the traditional Ayahuasca brew.

There is another very recent research that also seems to corroborate in some way my hypothesis, and also Leadbeater's clairvoyant observations.

It has this time nothing to do with shamanism but comes from a core physics research. It is William A. Tiller's highly innovating research on the power of intent involved in the transformation of matter.

In his book *Conscious Acts of Creation*, and the DVD with the same title, Dr. Tiller, Stanford University Professor Emeritus, claims that there is ample evidence for the fact that conscious and condensed thought, and intent impact upon matter, and actually change matter.

DVD Back Cover Text

> Based upon years of detailed research, Dr. Tiller has amassed convincing experimental data showing that in seemingly the same cognitive space, basic chemical reactions and basic material properties can be strongly altered by human intentions. Essentially, he says, we are all capable of performing what we typically think of as miracles.

If our intent projected upon time and space creates what Leadbeater and others call *elementals* or if it creates *thought–forms* or if it creates a collapsing of the wave function, to use an expression of quantum physics, really does not matter. We might as well call it magic thought power or telepathy. What imports is that we see that there is no magic other than the impact of spirit upon visible and tangible reality.

When I extrapolate this research that is amply documented by additional research in the meantime, then I must conclude that shamanic power is more than the mechanistic ingestion of plant chemistry 'to make things happen'. Then I will see that it's the preparation of the concoction much more than its chemical ingredients that make for the outcome of the experience, and that's ultimately *intent projected into the subtle matrix of plant consciousness* that is the trigger here.

THE CONSCIOUSNESS THEORY

*

I shall discuss the theory that I bring forward in this paper using my own experience with Ayahuasca as a point of reference.

There are eight arguments for supporting my hypothesis that I will bring forward and illustrate with examples. These arguments are:

> ▸ 1) Preparation of the brew;

> ▸ 2) Trance lasting hours after extensive vomiting and diarrhea;

> ▸ 3) Effect of the shaman's use of cigarette smoke;

> ▸ 4) The shaman's *focusing his thoughts* on the client;

> ▸ 5) The *strange* reception;

▸   6) The *hypnotic view* of the shaman's face;

▸   7) Similarity with hypnosis used in natural healing;

▸   8) Similarity with hypnosis used in psychiatry.

Let me now discuss each of these points.

1) The Ayahuasca Preparation

Upon my question about the details of the preparation of the brew, it is highly interesting what the shaman conveyed to me the morning after my arrival in Misahualli, Ecuador.

We had been discussing the religious nature of the Ayahuasca experience and Jimela, his assistant, was talking about her husband *Rafal*, a Polish businessman who, from what they said, appeared to be a prototype of a skeptic. For him, the plant simply contained a chemical that brings about certain psychedelic effects in the human brain, and it was all a matter of ingesting that chloride so as to experience the consciousness-altering effects.

Interestingly, from what I was told, things worked out in a way to firmly contradict his positivistic worldview. After several attempts to convince Rafal of proper *set and setting*, and the necessity of careful preparation of the religious experience, Esteban and Jimela said they had given up on him and let him prepare the brew by himself.

The occasion soon was given through the reception of several business friends from Poland that Rafal wanted to initiate in the Ayahuasca experience. To everybody's surprise the ceremony ended with a total failure. Rafal complained later to Esteban that his friends *did not feel anything*. And Rafal himself, while having gone through the experience several times successfully when the brew was prepared, with all due care, by Esteban's mother, could not understand that the effect was practically zero this time, plus headache for several hours.

I was intrigued.

—How can that be? I asked Esteban.

—Well, he replied, you see it's not just a matter of cooking that stuff and reducing a large pot of the brew to a tiny cup that you later drink. It's not just concentrating that substance. It's much more.

—What more? I insisted.

—It's *respect*, basically. This respect must be shown in many ways. The tradition for example says that a woman who has her days must not be in the house, and the couple must not engage in intercourse during the time the brew is on the stove. Even the children must not make noise and preferably remain playing outside. And then, there is one more element. During the whole three to four hours the Ayahuasca is on the stove, the shaman must focus on the pot. His entire psychic energy must be *focused* upon the brew all along it's on the stove. He should not engage in any other thought, he should not leave the house, he should not have any leisure time and he should by all means not touch a woman. He must give his entire respect to the Ayahuasca until the moment it is ready.

—What does this imply practically? I asked.

—It implies that he concentrates his thought energy on the event. He is mentally preparing the event in the sense that he prays to the serpent, the *Boa Constrictor* which is the spirit of the Ayahuasca, to please provide a meaningful experience to the ones drinking the brew so that they may be guided on the right way. That means he will not quit the room where the stove is burning and he will kind of *court the brew* with his whole attention, caring for the fire, the right level of heat, and so on. He may smoke, but his mind must remain focused upon a positive outcome of the later experience.

He also must feel a sort of *reverence* toward the Ayahuasca spirit. It means that he really is pure in his intentions, and not doing it for money, for example, but with the intention to help people, either for their spiritual advancement, or for healing, depending which branch of shamanism he is personally adhering to.

While I found that some of the precepts Esteban mentioned were simply destined to assure that the tradition not be spoilt by the ignoramus using it as a showcase kind of thing, I listened very carefully when he spoke about the *focus* the shaman had to give to the brew, about the mantras he had to recite over the brew, about the prayers he had to say and over the energetic input he had to give to the brew in form of *total attention* and a stringent concentration of his thought energy upon the outcome of the experience.

2) THE LASTING TRANCE

The second interesting point in the experience is that after having vomited out completely the contents of my stomach, and very violently so, the effects of the trance lasted for several more hours.

I already felt sick after the first thirty minutes passed agreeably, went on my knees and experienced a rather painful purge because my chest and back muscles began to hurt intensely. It took at least half an hour until I was back in my chair. And even then, the vomiting reflex persisted while nothing was coming out any more, except small quantities of stomach saliva.

And every time I closed my eyes, all would restart as a meticulously working computer program. Closing my eyes was like a code contained in that software. When I closed my eyes, and not before, the intelligence namely asked me telepathically if I wished to restart; affirming silently, I was at once experiencing the slight visual effects again and the trance began to get hold of my body once more.

Unfortunately every time instead of being able to let myself get deeper and deeper into that agreeable state of numbness and comfort, something in me terribly resisted and built an annoying level of anxiety that I was absolutely unable to get rid of. The anxiety, then, in turn triggered the vomiting reflex. I was mentally very clear about it all and how it was setup altogether, and told Esteban several times that I understood my resistance to the brew as a psychological defense against self-abandonment; and yet I was unable to cope with that dreadful anxiety.

Esteban however had no advice for me except suggesting me to go back to my room and sleep, and I felt helpless, then, and kind of *guilty*. Why was I resisting?

This went on for several turns. Each turn I would call him for help and he would slowly get up from his chair, put one of his hands on my head, blow cigarette smoke in my face and give strokes to my luminous body with the feather, and this felt *great*. Interestingly, when he blew smoke in my face, the trance immediately vanished, even if I left my eyes closed. How could that be, as the DMT was all the time in my blood?

These few moments filled me with delight, with confidence, with positive feelings and a sense of well-being. And then I would thank him, he would go back to his chair and sink in his own trance, and all would get back to the former desperate condition, and the vomiting would restart.

And eventually I asked to be guided back to my room and even there, about one to two hours after I had vomited out the brew, the process would restart in just the same way as before, just upon closing my eyes as the signal to restart.

Sleeping was only possible in the early morning hours, after more than two hours of a virulent duplex reaction of my body: I got diarrhea and vomiting at the same time. I was once really laughing about it, while I felt so much pain and misery, because I was getting into a *rocking* movement between the toilet and the sink that were luckily quite close to each other. That was my Ayahuasca rock!

Only when I was *completely empty and pure*, I felt I was ready for sleep. And then it was really wonderful, like being in heaven, a wonderful dreamless sleep and a very happy *light* feeling when waking up in the early morning.

3) THE SHAMANIC TREATMENTS

How can it be that the treatments I received from the shaman could completely change my condition for the time they lasted?

As I said, they consisted of several elements some of which I have not yet mentioned:

- Putting his hand on top of my head for a moment;

- Gently blowing cigarette smoke into my face;

- Giving me *magnetic strokes* with a feather-like device;

- Chanting an *ikaro*, a magic chant.

There was a moment when I became aware that my terrible anxiety had to do with my early childhood, that I had been abandoned as a small baby several times, a fact that my mother, when I was already adult, more or less hesitantly told me once when she was drunk.

I felt a great sense of comfort from the care I got from the shaman and it seemed to me that this care contained the same *love* that a mother bestows on her baby and I was just absorbing that love as if I was a small helpless baby.

But scientifically speaking, if the hypothesis is true that the trance is induced by DMT, how can the effects of the trance completely stop, while the DMT is still in the blood, under the influence of a kind of psychosomatic energy treatment? If the trance was *only* induced by the DMT, as a linear kind of causation, there is hardly any even remotely logical reply to be found to this question.

However, from the perspective of my hypothesis that the plant is only a *passive matrix* absorbing and remitting, and perhaps amplifying as well, the thought energy received from the shaman, then what I am saying begins to make sense.

Truly, all the effects of the DMT ceased, including the disagreeable swindle that set in every time when I opened my eyes, and I left them open every time I got the treatment as I found it pacifying and nice, and liked to see the shaman in his traditional dress and his serious and caring allure when gently blowing me cigarette smoke in my face.

There was a tenderness in his simple silent movements that greatly contributed to comforting me and alleviate my anxiety.

But logically, if the shaman was the *agent* of the trance and not the DMT, or if it was both, if he was the primary agent of the trance using plant consciousness as a transmitter of his thought forms, it is clear that he could stop it at will and re-trigger it at any moment in time!

4) FOCUS AND INTENT

In our initial talk about the Ayahuasca experience at the morning upon my arrival, Esteban had addressed the issue of *focus and care* in dealing with his clients.

I think he wanted to come over as a serious practitioner of the shamanic science as there are today many charlatans, especially in the tourism-plagued areas in Peru and Ecuador.

And explaining me more about his work and attitude, he said he would very intensely focus upon the client when beginning the trance. I was intrigued and asked:

—Do you drink the Ayahuasca brew as well, or only the client?

He replied that it depended *on the wish of the client,* and if I wished him to drink the brew together with me, that was okay with him. I affirmed that I wished him to do that and asked him why he focused or concentrated upon the client after the latter had ingested the brew?

He said he focused his mind on the client in order to help him better access the *boa spirit,* the mother spirit of the Ayahuasca, as he himself had been in touch with this spirit from the start, and that this was after all the precondition to being a shaman.

Thus, consciously remembering this conversation with Esteban, I tightly observed him when we started the ceremony, and indeed, after we had drunk the brew from the beautifully carved traditional silver cups, he was sitting down not like me in the beach chair, stretched out and relaxed, but in a fetal forward position that suggested to me he was *concentrating on something.*

And he remained in that position for a long time, actually as long as the preparation lasted, the time before the DMT begins to being absorbed by the body and deploy its effect—which is about thirty to forty minutes.

Then, when I felt the trance began, he was stretching out in the chair in a more relaxed position.

And I think that even for a third observer this connection of events, this *Gestalt* as it were, would suggest the hypothesis that it's the shaman who is the primary trigger of the experience, and not just some chlorides in a plant concoction.

5) THE STRANGE RECEPTION

Upon entering the hut, I saw three human figures in beach chairs and did not recognize them. I was *unable* to recognize who they were, as if my thoughts were seized by an unknown power, or as if there was an overlay over my thinking process. I felt I was floating.

Please note that at that moment I had just come from my room, refreshed after some sleep, and yet suddenly, upon entering the place where the ritual was going to take place, I felt dominated by an alien force.

I have never had memory lapses or anything even remotely close to a lack of memory for human faces. I have a very good memory for human faces, even after long years to have known a person, and meeting her again. But here, there is no valid reason to be found why I did not recognize the three persons sitting there.

Something like that never happened to me before. I felt as if under the influence of something that rendered me incapable of assessing the reality of the simple scene I was facing. It was just after sunset, and it was not yet dark, around eight in the evening. The distance between them and me was not more than five or six meters, not more and perhaps less.

The strangeness or queerness of the moment was the fact that I did not *feel* their presence. It was as if there were humans present but that these humans were strangely *disconnected* from me. And they did not invite me to come closer and just remained silent, and I felt like an idiot, not knowing what to do, not knowing what to say.

Eventually, feeling really *embarrassed*, I asked if they knew where Jimela and Esteban were? And only then the female got up from her chair and approached me and I saw it was Jimela.

When I apologized for not having recognized them upon entering the hut, they said it did not matter, but to me it mattered a lot!

How could something like that happen? It remains a mystery to me until this day.

I namely evaluate this event as an overlay of consciousness. Already at that moment the shaman tried to get into my consciousness interface, and he did this by what he said he always did when preparing for accompanying a client on an Ayahuasca trip: he *focused* on the client's consciousness. This focusing on the client simply was a native variation of what in Western medical science we call hypnosis. He had *hypnotized* me, even before I had taken in a drop of the Ayahuasca brew.

And this is essentially the core of my hypothesis. And as I am not a newcomer to hypnosis, because otherwise I would probably not have discovered this intriguing explanation of how shamanism works, I erect this now as a theory and ask scientists for evaluating it by either corroborating or falsifying it.

I will honestly relate in this paper my earlier experiences with hypnosis both in the setting of natural healing and in the medical hypnosis setting.

6) THE HYPNOTIC VIEW

Strangely, when I was in trance, I saw the shaman's face differently. I guess this experience would frighten someone with lesser paranormal knowledge and experience.

His face seemed distorted, ugly and diabolic. His mouth was shifted to the right, open and white inside. And this strange mouth did not move while I heard Esteban talking, and even talking quite fast, so fast that I wanted to tell him to talk more slowly because my understanding of Spanish, while normally quite good, was reduced in trance, but finally I did not get a word out and just remained silent.

I remembered my experiences with hypnosis and especially the one I went through with the quite extraordinary female German healer that I will report further down.

Needless to add that this *strangeness* about Esteban's face resulted only in increasing my anxiety and discomfort about the whole of the Ayahuasca experience.

7) HYPNOSIS AND NATURAL HEALING

It is important to retain here that hypnosis itself was not at all something strange or alien to me because I have had quite extensive experience with it in the past, and I think it is very important that I relate this experience shortly.

To repeat it, without this experience, I do not think I would so easily have come up with the present hypothesis; I would probably have accepted my Ayahuasca experience as a queer one and forgotten about it.

Now, let me be very precise what I am talking about. I am talking here about *medical hypnosis*, not about *stage hypnosis*.

There is almost a world of difference between both forms of hypnosis. Medical hypnosis is a form of auto-hypnosis in the sense that it builds upon the full consent of the patient and his active participation in the progression of the trance, while in stage hypnosis the willpower of the individual or the entire audience that is hypnotized is as good as put to zero.

Let me illustrate this a little further. It is recognized in the meantime that, for example, the acrobatic trick of *sawing the woman* can be done in two different ways. The traditional way was to hypnotize the entire audience and *suggest* to them what they were going to see, as for example the woman cut in two, who yet afterwards leaves the box unhurt.

As stage hypnosis has been *discredited* as a form of abuse and also because the art of stage hypnosis was an orally transmitted knowledge and got more and more lost with the disappearance of the *circus* as an institution, today, in almost all cabarets, when you see the *sawing the woman* trick, it's a simple trickster effect you are succumbing to. And yet still today a famous popular figure such as *David Copperfield* admits that part of his magic is hypnosis, and not only tricking the audience out with visual and sensory effects, immense speed of action, and uncanny ways to act.

Thus, the two experiences of hypnosis that I wish to relate here, and the further ones that I will report in the next paragraph exclusively deal with medical hypnosis, and not with stage hypnosis. And it goes without saying that I do not suspect Esteban to be a charlatan, but an integer shaman who applies, as exactly as possible, a tradition that he shares with several tribes of Shuar natives, and that he learnt from an old and experienced senior shaman.

The two experiences of hypnosis that I will relate are quite different while both can be qualified as medical hypnosis. Their difference is that in the first experience the hypnosis was a person-to-person one, while in the second experience the hypnosis was a person-to-group one and thus a form of collective hypnosis.

The first experience was taking place back in 1997, when I had just returned to Germany from an exhausting two-year business trip to South-East Asia, with my intestinal flora completely down. I had gone through severe episodes of diarrhea and intense dehydration over months and was at that time still consulting Western doctors who prescribed me huge amounts of antibiotics to fight the diarrhea.

The result was that the diarrhea continued despite all but my intestinal flora was completely destroyed by the long-term antibiotics treatment. I was suffering from chronic fatigue and felt very lethargic, lacking motivation and appetite. It was for this reason that I consulted a *homeopathic healer* for help. I got several effective treatments and one of them, the one I remember most vividly, was a treatment with the famous *Bach flower essences.*

The female practitioner who had told me she had studied hypnosis and Reiki with a powerful Filipino healer, first wanted to choose the right Bach flower essence for me and my problem. She explained me very patiently the various methods for finding the energy essence corresponding to my organism's *energy code* and asked me which one I preferred. I chose the most direct one, the one that is done through hypnosis, and the experience was going to be a particularly revealing one for me.

She was sitting at a forty-five degree angle at my right and asked me to put my left hand in her right hand. Then she told me to look in her eyes while she would take one flacon after the other in her left hand to *sense* the effect the vibration of the plant essence had on my organism. Never before was I hypnotized so easily, so effectively and so joyfully. It was a very agreeable condition and I felt very clearly how each of the essences impacted energetically upon me.

She said I was going to feel either joyful, peaceful, positive and happy, which indicated that the essence was right for me, or I was feeling queer, anxious and negative, which was indicating that the essence was not compatible with my aura's vibrational structure. Now, what I wish to report about this experience is something really unusual and that I would call *the hypnotic view.*

What I want to say is that from the moment I was hypnotized I realized that my *perception of ordinary reality shifted* and I saw things differently, in a distorted way, or I even saw things that we ordinarily never see. And what I found most amazing was that I saw on the front of my healer a *huge third eye*, as real as it could ever be, a very intelligent-looking large human eye that did not in the least frighten me. In the contrary, in that special hypnotic condition I knew and acknowledged that I saw her *third eye*, her sixth chakra, only that in this special view I could visualize this eye that all the old mythologies abound of telling us.

And I told her at once about my discovery and she was not the least astonished. She said that other patients had seen it as well and that it was quite a normal experience for her, and that according to her Filipino teacher it showed that she had a great innate potential for healing—and this was really true as her treatment was the most effective one can imagine.

It was almost miraculous. I was completely cured within three months, and with only six sessions.

Two years later I started off to another fascinating healing experience, this time directly with a Filipino healer. At that time the magazines in Germany were full of reports about Filipino healers and the photos were absolutely dumbfounding. I saw that the healer had both his hands deep within the belly of a female patient and that there was blood all around, so much blood, and that suddenly he took out something from her intestines, something like a black stone, and threw it on the floor and declared to have found the *evil* in her body. I really thought it was all a dirty trick and wanted to know the truth about it.

Thus I signed up when a befriended natural healer from Hamburg called me and invited me for an audience in a naturopathy practice in Frankfurt where I was going to meet one of the most powerful Filipino healers.

While I have studied quite a bit of parapsychology over the years, already during my law studies, I was very skeptical regarding this kind of healing. I told to myself I'd be very watchful to find out what was their trick, while I thought to myself that the soundest hypothesis for all this to happen simply was group hypnosis.

However I was struck by the fact that this hypnosis can affect photographic plates as well, and be taken on video. So, after all, can it be explained with group hypnosis? I had seen this in those magazines even before I went to Frankfurt, and thus it was possible to photograph something that is not to explain within our present reality paradigm. It is and remains a miracle until this day.

I plead for the hypnosis theory here simply because I was experienced with medical hypnosis already and knew how it *felt* and how ordinary perception reacts to it. Because it's really that once you have experienced hypnosis, you know for all times *how it feels* when somebody tries to hypnotize you. You are *aware* that you are being hypnotized in a certain moment, and you can fight it if you don't wish to succumb to it, however pleasurable it may feel. Let me add that indeed, generally, it feels very pleasurable if your general anxiety level is not, like mine at that time, higher than average and you build a resistance against it.

Now, they seemed to try everything to avoid resistance when we were comfortably installed in that natural healer's practice in Frankfurt. We were being thoroughly prepared for the experience, during more than two hours, during which the healer was still busy with another group. We did not see him and had to remain in a special meeting room where we were being instructed about the strictly spiritual principles that traditional Filipino healers are bound to.

We were really well informed and I got to know the first names of most of the participants that were women in their great majority.

The atmosphere in the group was friendly and amicable and I felt really relaxed when we entered the room where I saw the healer on the floor, near to a bed and next to a vessel with burning incense. He seemed to be in a deep state of prayer and meditation. In the room several pictures showing the *Holy Virgin* and *Jesus the Christ* were hanging on the walls, and the audience was visibly collected and in a state of respect and awe upon entering the room.

During the whole experience I did not feel the slightest discomfort or fear and I wish to state this right at the start of this report because it so sharply contrasts with my Ayahuasca experience. Then, all went exactly as I had seen it reported in the magazines. The healer called one of the women to the bed and let her stretch out comfortably, asking her to slightly open the belt of her trousers or skirt so that he could plainly touch her abdomen.

By the way, none of the women felt the slightest discomfort at this demand of the healer. His requesting her to take off her shirt equally did not result in any resistance. Then he *opened* her belly by the navel entry, and virtually penetrated into the navel with the fingers of his right hand, until the navel was an open hole of about the size of the healer's fist.

This opening bled abundantly, and the healer then introduced both of his hands through the navel hole until deep in the woman's intestines.

He seemed to search for something in there. Several times, he extruded a part of the large or small intestines, looked at them or rubbed them. He appeared to search for something particular and almost in every case he found it: it was objects like small stones, most of the time of black color, and when he got one he threw it visibly and audibly on the floor.

One of the most interesting details is namely that upon awakening from our collective hypnosis, not only was there no blood anywhere, but there were absolutely no stones to be found on the floor!

Then the woman who was sitting to my left was called. She was a nice young lady who had complained in our previous talks about a problem with digestion that lasted over many years and that she thought could not be cured with Western medicine, as she had *tried everything already*. With her, the treatment took longer than with any other participant and she seemed to suffer from it, was howling two times very deeply from the depth of her body, like a hurt animal, and gave me a deep regard when she returned, saying:

—I feel *very* hurt, I am suffering great pain!

I was kind of shocked, so much the more as I was called as the next patient. But in my case all went fine and I did not feel anything and avoided to open my eyes, somewhat afraid I could be shocked to see blood, yet did not feel any pain. And upon returning to my seat, I immediately asked her if she had seen me bleeding and she replied that, yes, I had been bleeding abundantly and that the healer had put his two hands in my intestines but that in my case the treatment had been a lot shorter than with most of the other patients, and especially herself.

I was asking her then if her pain was less and she said that indeed, the pain was gradually decreasing, giving rise to a feeling of comfort that she had not experienced since many years.

Later we were discussing and exchanging about this daring experience but never got a chance to talk directly to the healer. However, the naturopath and owner of the practice offered a free consultation and revealed to be a very good initiate into this practice that he had learned from several Filipino healers.

Thus, we all left that experience with a great feeling of delight and amazement, and I can only say with Goethe that school knowledge will not suffice to explain this extraordinary form of healing.

To avoid a misunderstanding, let me be very clear and to the point: I do *not* say that healing induced by hypnosis, related to hypnosis or which may be a veiled form of hypnosis was charlatanism or was not effective. In the contrary!

What I say is that healing which seems *miraculous* to us is in fact a treatment that is so effective that we can't believe it when we compare it to our ordinary, and rather palliative, healing methods. I further say that this *effectiveness* is due to *suggestion* and that suggestion is a command that uses the *power of the word* to impact upon the condition of the body. The only difference between the normal waking state and the hypnotic state is that in the latter, the body is more suggestible.

Now, what most people don't want to see is that the healing brought about by suggestion is by no means fake healing, but healing that is as good or even better than ordinary healing.

Sometimes we understand certain things when we look at their contrary, or their negative side. So let me give an example that demonstrates what I am saying. It is an old experiment and has been repeated often by *Milton Erickson* to demonstrate the power of hypnosis as a verbal suggestion that directly *impacts* upon the soma. The patient is in deep hypnosis and is told by the hypnotherapist that a sizzling hot iron will be applied to her arm for a few seconds.

Then, the therapist takes the iron which is of course cold, and applies it to the patient's arm. Immediately the body reacts *is if the iron was really burning hot*, and builds a huge watering blister. This blister is still present when the patient wakes up and it takes the same time to heal out as if she was really burnt. It goes without saying that she also experienced some local pain and had to give her full consent before engaging in that really dumbfounding experiment.

Now imagine that what can be done negatively to the body through verbal suggestion can as well done to it *positively*. This explains that under hypnosis healing can be instantaneous and totally effective!

The most important to report in our context is the similarity in the way the hypnotic trance manifests. You will read about it again in the next paragraph regarding medical hypnosis used in psychiatry. Let me summarize so far that this trance usually begins in the arms with a relaxation of the hand and lower arm muscles and then gradually mounts upwards into the body, passing region by region like a gentle embrace, thus the upper arms, the shoulders, the face and head, then the chest and the muscles around the heart.

The fear block I experienced was located in my heart region and this already had been confirmed by the homeopathic healer in Germany who, after an extended treatment, told me that from my earliest childhood I had suffered a problem with being abandoned and that my heart chakra was closed, whereupon she opened it by slightly touching my heart region with her finger. This slight touch triggered an amazing amount of tears and I suddenly remembered early childhood feelings and went through a really difficult moment during about one hour, upon which I was left in total peace and serenity, feeling like *newborn*.

To summarize, I reacted very differently during the inducement of the hypnotic trance.

In two instances, with the Filipino healer and the German homeopath, it was a very agreeable and smooth experience, while when I did it with psychiatrists, it was rather anxiety-creating. And with the Ayahuasca it was frightening as well.

I conclude that the fact to experience fear or not depends on the hypnotizer and not the particular kind of hypnosis he uses. I tend to believe, and I am open to change my opinion if it should reveal as scientifically unsound, that hypnosis requires a high amount of immediate trust between the patient and the hypnotherapist or shaman, or natural healer. When this trust is lacking, anxiety will interfere with the depth of the hypnosis or make it a rather disagreeable negative experience.

8) MEDICAL HYPNOSIS

The first time I experienced medical hypnosis was in 1989, in Geneva, with a quite famous transactional and Gestalt therapist, Dr. Margareta Robinson.

It was the first time that I ever got in touch with hypnosis, and unfortunately I was *not informed* that it was hypnosis that I was going to experience! When she presented her approach to me, Mrs. Robinson was talking about a combination of transactional and Gestalt therapy that she seemed to have melted into a powerful approach for healing various problems from neuroses to narcissism.

I was surprised at the ease of how that hypnosis was brought about. It was by means of using a pet, a *teddy bear*. Indeed, upon holding that magic pet I felt a deep and very *sad* kind of relaxation affecting my body and mind. I suddenly felt extremely tired, and powerless; that sensation was not at all joyful and agreeable, but an experience that left me very depressive. I began to feel apathetic and helpless, *very powerless*, like a baby abandoned at the mercy of some or the other untrustworthy caretaker.

My arm muscles became weaker and weaker, as if I was given a sleep potion, until I could not lift my arms up any more.

Then she asked me to get up, handed me a tennis racket and said:

—Here on this couch your mother is stretched out. She is sleeping. Hit her with this racket as much as you like! And I could not do it and told her about it. She said:

—Well, this proves only your problem to me. You have internalized all the violence and resistance against your mother and are for the moment unable to exteriorize it. That's why you suffer from depressions. They indicate the deep hatred against your mother and we would have to work on releasing this energy.

I did not agree with her and her approach. I felt she was pushing the therapy in a very hurried and jumpy way that was not bringing me relief while I must say that when coming home from each session, I felt I was seeing the world literally with other eyes, so much all seemed to have changed for the better.

I then began a hypnotherapy with an American therapist and this therapy progressed much more carefully, while I must admit that we never entered a really deep level of hypnosis because of the fear problem I already described earlier in this report.

SUMMARY

The experience with *Ayahuasca* as I made it with the Shuar shaman back in 2004 is in my view supportive for a non-linear and multi-causative, rather than a linear and single-causative theory of cognition regarding the psychedelic visions and insights subsequent to ingesting the traditional brew.

In addition, in my discussions with the shaman and his assistant, equally a Shuar native, it appeared clear that they themselves rejected the linear and single-causative theory of the kind stating 'it's the DMT that makes for all that Ayahuasca does,' explaining that all the art was in the traditional procedure of preparing the cure and the consciousness focus that forms part of it.

In fact, the negative experience of the Polish businessman with the brew, and the resulting ineffectiveness of it, shows evidently that the single-causative linear theory of cognition regarding the Ayahuasca is flawed.

The cognitive experience with Ayahuasca is probably not a simple direct consequence of the plant-containing DMT, as this has been suggested, for example, by Terence McKenna and his brother, the ethnobotanist Dennis McKenna in their book *The Invisible Landscape (1994)*.

In the eight specific particularities that I have brought forward and commented on in the previous chapter, there appears to be a certain weight of the evidence for a causation of the cognitive experience by shamanic consciousness acting as a hypnotic agent on the plant matrix that serves as a resilient *transmitter and amplifier of thought energy.*

The specific cognitive elucidation and the insights experienced after ingestion of the brew, that I shall report in more detail in the following last chapter, are brought about through a multi-causative impact of the consciousness imprint on my own consciousness interface. This impact was brought about through the strong focus of the shaman's thought energies on my perception matrix and reception frequency both during the preparation of the brew and at the onset of the intake ritual.

This concentration of thought and attention is known both from parapsychological research and clairvoyant experience, and from medical hypnosis to bring about an energy imprint in form of a *consciousness overlay* on the perception interface of the receiver.

I am talking about a multi-causative effect here because the evidence at stake does not allow to exclude any *proprietary additional impact* of the plant consciousness in the process of triggering the consciousness overlay.

In fact, there are details in my report that indicate such an additional impact directly from the side of the plant realm, as a *genuine plant-proprietary consciousness* reaching out into my human consciousness.

The most striking detail in this context was that I had myself the clear intuition of being in touch with a proprietary *plant consciousness* or even an unspecific *universal consciousness* that I was in an ongoing telepathic exchange with as long as the trance lasted, and that I was, strangely enough, in state of turning that telepathic communication on and off by simply closing or opening my eyes.

In addition, the obvious parallels with my previous hypnosis-induced alterations of consciousness demonstrate that the focusing of thought energy that the shaman did as a preparation for the ritual in accordance with traditional native tradition has in some way to do with hypnosis, or brings about an effect or imprint on another's consciousness that is similar to a hypnotic injunction.

The most important detail in this context is well the fact that there is a *plant-specific matrix* involved in this process, and not just a shaman focusing thought energy on myself as his client. This is the specific contextual link with plant consciousness acting as a matrix receiver for intent, similar as this has been reported for water, by the elucidating research of the Japanese researcher Masaru Emoto.

As Emoto's water research suggests, it is possible to leave imprints in the memory interface of water by positive or negative affirmations, for example in the form of textual labels glued on the water bottles for some time, that produce or not in the water specific crystals.

Typically so, the aesthetically appealing crystals are formed by positive and uplifting intent and correlated affirmations rather than by negative and defeating intent and affirmations.

My argument here with regard to the cognitive imprints received in the form of insights during an Ayahuasca trip is on the same lines of reasoning. My idea is that the consciousness interface of plants, at least of plants that are qualified as *entheogens* or as plants containing mind-altering compounds, serves as a transmitting and amplifying interface for the thought imprint given to it by the shaman's consciousness and thought energy.

In how much the plant here participates with its own consciousness-altering compounds, such as DMT, cannot be evaluated from this experience with Ayahuasca, but needs additional, tightly curtailed research. It is namely possible that the plant chemistry, instead of being a unilateral agent of altering human consciousness, serves as a receiver, transmitter and amplifier interface for human intent and thought energy, as this has been reported by Masaru Emoto and others for the *hado*, the specific energy-interface of water.

But even Masaru Emoto has not found, and not even tried to explain the ultimate reason why human intent can have an energetic impact on water, and other substances.

The explanation, or one possible explanation, is given by Charles Webster Leadbeater in his 1894 booklet *Astral Plane* where he describes the function of elementals in the communication between humans and all realms of nature.

—Charles W. Leadbeater, Astral Plane (1894).

Leadbeater explains that thought is an energetic phenomenon that creates certain vibrations, called thought forms or *elementals*.

These elementals, he says further, gain permanence over time and depending on how much emotional energy we invest in those thoughts. And interestingly so, here we encounter the philosophy of the natives who speak about *spirits* when asked what the communicating agents were between humans and plants. And the solution of the riddle is to view the natives' explanation and the theosophical or clairvoyant view together.

The technique consists thus in imprinting intent in the plant matrix by gestating, through the power of thought energy, certain elementals that function as communicating agents between the human and the plant realm.

These elementals, I suppose, are created during the process of collecting the Ayahuasca liana and carefully preparing the brew, and it is these elementals impacting on the plants' psychoactive substances that are becoming active and *communicative* as it were in the initiate's consciousness.

And, to come to an end, I think what the contextual scope of the present Ayahuasca experience well indicates is that a simplistic linear cause-and-effect mechanism between

DMT and cognitive insights can safely be discarded as a theory.

Cognitive Experiences

＊

When asked to summarize the insights I got through the ingestion of *Ayahuasca*, I can establish the following catalog—

- The intelligence's *alien* noise interface;

- The intelligence's *pulsation* as a cosmic energy;

- The intelligence's attempts to *calling me* in touch;

- Insights about my conditioning through language;

- Insights about relationships with others and the world;

- Insights about love and life.

These insights did not come up in my consciousness all at once, but rather through little chunks that were repeated several times and variations, extending virtually until the moment, early in the morning, when I feel asleep.

Interestingly so, the very last insights I got immediately before falling asleep, at around four o'clock in the morning, when already stretched out on my bed, after the *purga* eventually had stopped.

It was then that I was suddenly intensely aware of my solitude, my utter lack of relationships, and my general feeling of being disconnected from other people. And it was then that the insights about relationships and about love and life came through.

Another interesting detail is that most insights only came up after I had asked questions to myself or this specific intelligence I was in touch with, while I had not always formulated my questions as questions, but often as affirmations that were then propelled back to me like in a boomerang effect. And what happened was that most of the time the affirmations had been slightly altered in the process. I shall give examples.

ALIEN NOISE AND PULSATION

The first phenomenon I noticed about the specific intelligence I felt approaching right at the onset of the trance was its *alien noise*. This noise was clearly distinct from the frog concert and other natural sounds that surrounded me.

My senses were not dulled by the trance but in the contrary sharpened and I could clearly distinguish between the multitude of natural sounds around me in the clear evening air, and the specific alien noise of this intelligence.

When I should put it in words, which is somehow an impossible quest because of the paranormal reality as the contextual background, I would say it's like many, thousands or millions of human voices simultaneously whispering a mantra. I think it is an important detail that it's not just like a machine noise, or a tone, but that it bears a resemblance to a whispering human voice multiplied by the millions.

I know that Terence McKenna has spoken of the *machine elves* and their *alien sound* as a typical manifestation during the DMT-induced trance. But what I am saying is that in contradistinction to McKenna's perception, the sound was *not* machine-like but came over to me as *organic*, and somehow related to nature.

I call it *alien* only because there is no sound or anything you could have ever heard in your wake life that bears any similitude to this sound. Actually I prefer the term *noise* over sound because noise is a term used in telecommunications, as something that can either be a background hiss, such as the hiss on vinyl records, or a certain unspecific hum contained in ultra-short wave receivers, or else it's a term used by graphics designers for the lacking smoothness of an image. All these connotations fit here, in my opinion.

The presence of the *natural intelligence* of the Ayahuasca spirit is related to sound as it manifests not visually in the first place, but audibly, and thus it bears an impact of *resonance.*

It has to do with vibration, and with frequency. It has to do with cell resonance and with Sheldrake's notion of *morphic resonance,* as it resonates the mix of nature's frequencies, and comes over as the *Universal Communicator,* and at the same time, the Universal Bearer of all these energies.

—See, for example, Rupert Sheldrake, A New
Science of Life (1995).

This is exactly what I wanted to convey
actually about the *organic quality* of the
sound: to me it bears a morphological
resemblance with organic life, and organic
sounds, only that it overlays many or a
multitude of such sounds in its audible
presence.

So, as with ultra-wave communication, the
Ayahuasca intelligence comes through on a
certain frequency, and not on another, and the
frequency is tuned by ingesting the brew, and
here the DMT may well be active as the
attunement agent.

From the onset of the trance, the alien
noise was gradually rising in volume, and after
some time, I clearly understood that this
sound was something like the *pulsation* of the
universe, or life, and in that moment I got an

intense awareness of the fact that all creation is in fact a result of *sound*, and that life intrinsically is vibration, is sound.

This is an insight that I have well today acquired through having studied hermetic and modern literature on sound used for healing, but years ago, when I went through this experience, I was not yet consciously aware of this fact.

Hence, I can say that this insight was novelty for me. And yet, it sounded completely sound and solid, so to speak, and did not come as a surprise. It is as if the intelligence had not just communicated me something using telepathic touch, but as if it had subtly awakened my intelligence to a novel insight that from that moment could not be unthought any more from my consciousness.

THE FIVE DEPTH LEVELS

From the onset of the Ayahuasca trance, I got clear telepathic messages that I should go beyond that first phase during which I saw subtle geometric forms that bore however much of a lesser brilliance and luminosity than those I had seen in some research volumes, such as Pablo Amaringo's *Ayahuasca Visions* (1999). And I knew in that moment that, contrary to what I had learnt and heard from others about the Ayahuasca trip, the visions were of no importance at all. I simply *knew* this or it was communicated to me in that moment.

At the same time I was called upon by the intelligence to go beyond that first rather insignificant level and explore into the next depth level, but that for getting there I needed to *relax more* and let go some of the fear that I felt was like a congested knot in my heart chakra. The intelligence also communicated to me that there were in total *five depth levels* in the Ayahuasca experience.

I think it is significant to note that I found this in none of the books I had read when doing my research on shamanism and entheogens, and I have not found it subsequent to my experience in any additional books I read about the Ayahuasca quest. What I have well learnt from Michael Harner's seizing account of his own primary Ayahuasca trip, during which he almost died, in his book *Ways of the Shaman (1990)*, was that he had himself experienced, right from the start, the toughest depth level—encountering the primal dragons. But neither Harner nor other researchers and experiencers have given an account of how many depth levels there are, while all seem to agree that there are in fact several levels of intensity to be possibly experienced during the psychedelic trip.

There is something like a *consensus doctorum* in the literature about the ritual use of entheogens that sets a relationship between dose of the substance intake to the intensity of the trip—and here I made a nice and meaningful typo, writing *insensity* instead of intensity. This is true in so far as the experience gets weirder and apparently more insane as a result of our cherished assumptions about reality, and the *sense* that we give to certain experiences being shifted in the course of the strong psychedelic experience.

However, I want to warn here again falling in the trap of single causality and of linear thinking when it goes to evaluate a type of experiences that is intrinsically multi-causal and nonlinear in character. In my view, the *depth levels* that Ayahuasca contains are probably not triggered by the dose alone, but also by the *intensity of the focus and intent* bestowed upon the brew from the side of the shaman.

Now, what is also rather uncanny and that I have not found in any description of Ayahuasca trips anywhere in a book is that the intelligence gave me *signals*. It was like a gentle knocking at my doors of perception. I typically saw a flickering of five red squares at the top upper left corner of my vision, when my eyes were closed.

I intuitively knew in these moments that this was the signal to go deeper in the trance, or jump to the next depth level, only that to my sadness I could not follow the invitation because of my fear block. Every time it happened, the fear came up and blocked me to go beyond. And this blockage was not just mental. If it had been mental only I could have overcome it. In fact, I wanted to overcome it, but then the blockage somatized and manifested as vomiting, and later also as strong diarrhea. It was not only my mind that resisted the experience, but also, and perhaps primarily so, my body.

CALLING ME IN TOUCH

I was *constantly communicating* with the intelligence, from the first to the last moment of my Ayahuasca experience. I had prayed already before the onset of the experience, while still on my bed in my hotel room, that through this wisdom quest I might receive guidance for finding my life's mission and for being freed from my constant anxiety, and I kept addressing the Ayahuasca spirit in respectful terms during the experience to assist me in my quest for truth.

And as if it was a final test that this intelligence really understood me, I said this, when I felt I wanted to go back to my room and sleep:

MY SILENT PRAYER

Dear Ayahuasca Spirit, thank you so much for all the insights, please stop calling me now. I know that I was not able to get over my fear block now, and I hope I can find the courage to continue because I know you will reveal me so much more when I get deeper in the trance. But for now I have decided to stop. It is enough.

And immediately the *calling* stopped, the flickering lights did not appear anymore and the alien noise was calming down and stopped as well.

This alien noise, I understood then, was the *language* of that intelligence. It was something like many people, in some distance, speaking simultaneously, and as if many conversations converged to a chaotic no-sense that was but the secret code or pattern of a deeper, much more unified language of the universe, and of which our human language is only a tiny and almost insignificant part.

FREEING FROM CONDITIONING

The plant intelligence I was in touch with seemed to convey to me telepathically that I was *locked* in language, that all my experiencing of life was conditioned upon language, and that I hardly ever perceived life *directly*, spontaneously, as an immediate connection.

At the same time, I received the instant confirmation that this intelligence was *universal* in the sense that it was connected to all, and that it was constantly trying to connect all, such as a total communication matrix of the universe; and third that it was and represented all-that-is.

I became keenly aware that this intelligence was the *Logos*, and that it simply *was*, and it gently invited me to enter this connection, this wonderful all-encompassing love that it irradiated and communicated.

Several times, when I intended to tell the shaman some of my cognitive experiences while still in trance, the intelligence seemed to wanting to hold me back. Once I wanted to say something regarding the intelligence, and I was stopped in midst of the sentence:

—*Este inteligencia* ..., was all that I could say.

The intelligence seemed to wanting to free me from the conditioning I had received through language, and through using language for describing reality.

It might be that my fear is in some way connected to language and my fear block a hypertrophy of language or of my left brain.

This is how I can try to explain it while all what I write here and can express in words never can come close to the actual experience.

LOVE, LIFE AND RELATIONSHIPS

Before I come to talk about the important insights I received about love, life and relationships at the end of my Ayahuasca trip, I would like to expand a little on that peculiar question-and-answer game that was developing between the intelligence and myself.

In fact, I was naturally the one who, puzzled, asked the questions, and the intelligence always *instantly* replied. When I say instantly I really mean that the reply did not even take one second to appear, but it was instantly in my mind upon formulating the question.

I think this is quite uncanny as a fact while it is probably known to other researchers.

And the reply could have various forms. It was always economical in the sense that it never wasted even one syllable, and when this was possible, it was just turning around my question, or simply *shortened* it, in order to give the answer. This is something I really have never heard of before, and it reminded me of a higher evolution of certain circus jokes or mind games, and it definitely had a note of humor to it.

The most important experience in this context was that my questions were *somehow returned as* questions-that-question-again-my-questions, so as to give the answer to any question as a result of the question itself—and not as some kind of outside input.

So in a way, the phenomenon suggested that the intelligence I was communicating with was altogether *not* an outside or outward or distinct intelligence, but simply a part of my own higher consciousness.

Now, succinctly speaking, this manifested in a way that every thought I had was immediately *returned to its contrary* and every phrase that I pronounced in my mind was immediately reduced to some more general insight.

For example I heard myself thinking:

—I love life …

And it was immediately reduced to:

—I *love* …

Or I heard myself thinking:

—I feel to be alive …

And it was reduced to:

—I *feel* …

And now, when you evaluate the returned, condensed or shortened statements *as answers*, you will notice that they are indeed highly intelligent answers to underlying questions.

The first statement could be read as an underlying question of the kind: 'What does it mean to love life?'

Now from the returned shortened version, it becomes evident that when I love, I simply love—which means I am in a state of love, and thus as a result I love all-that-is, and thus *also* life. So it's somehow unintelligent to say a sentence like 'I love life' because love cannot be reduced to just a concept like 'love of life' or it is that: *a concept and not love anymore.*

By the same token, to divide love off in concepts such as filial love, passionate love, love for children or love for the elder does not make sense, as what it produces is splitting the holistic notion of love off in tidy compartments that are *concepts of love*, but not *love* anymore.

So somehow the intelligence politely corrected what I was saying without correcting me! And I immediately understood the hint, like when you solve a *koan* in Zen.

—I use the expression koan in my books in order to denote the paradoxes that are the outcome of our intellectual, conceptual look at life. However, please be aware that I am convinced that life or nature is not per se paradoxical, but bound together in infinite harmony. The paradoxical nature of life is an appearance of reality made up through our limited, concept-based and thought-created image of reality—and not reality itself.

Eventually I became very quiet and full of gratitude and I said this in my thought, in my German mother tongue:

—*Ich möchte Liebe!* (I want love)

And immediately the response was, in German:

—*Ich möchte lieben …* (I want to love)

And with all my heart and soul I understood this subtle difference and it was clear to me that in this tiny difference of syntax there was *all the difference.*

It was the secret to happiness!

I had taken love as a commodity that can be received, stating that I wanted to be loved, instead of understanding that love was not something to receive, but a state of being to develop into, something like an attitude, and this attitude, it seemed to me, simply was total openness.

And at the same moment I became intensely and acutely aware that I was not in that state of love, that I was not giving love to others, and I also knew *why!* It was fear that blocked me off to love. And Krishnamurti's saying came to mind that for the first time I really understood: *where fear is, love cannot be.* And I think this insight transformed something in me. And really, afterwards my relationships changed much for the better.

Literature Review

*

The first book I read on the subject of shamanism in the 1980s was *Les appeleurs d'âmes* by Sabine Hargous, a French ethnologist. This study published in 1975 with the well-known French publisher *Albin Michel* and that translates in English as *The Soul Callers* is a well-documented thesis on the shamanic universe of the Andine native population.

This book clearly centers on one aspect of shamanism only: the healing. The study divides into three main parts *Indigenous Pathogenics*, *Diagnostics* and *Magic Rituals*. However, implicitly, the author expands on virtually all aspects of shamanic spirituality.

After all, it was perhaps a good thing to have begun with this study and not with something that conveys a *felt sense* of indigenous living, as for example the excellent books of Michael Harner, because Sabine Hargous' approach represents decidedly a Western view, with all that this implies.

She calls natives *primitives*, as it was the custom in traditional ethnology and that says in one word more than a whole thesis about what quantum physics has taught us about *the observer bias*. But for this reason the study is not to be discarded. I would even say this consciousness split is important for some people who else would never read a similar study because their anxiety to remain firmly rooted in their own cultural belief system is greater than their curiosity to explore other, and certainly more direct methods to approach reality.

And as, at this time, I was still working on my international law doctorate and not yet on the daring path to question the Western science approach—while I became more and more critical to it—this was certainly a good book to begin with. As the author was keeping her Cartesian distance to an alternative worldview, she was nonetheless getting deeply immersed in the world of the natives, and her book is all but a dry thesis paper.

The next book that virtually fell in my hands, as I found it on a garage sale, was Michael Harner's bestseller *Ways of the Shaman (1980/1982)*. This book had a different impact upon me than the first one. It was a shock and a revealing new learning!

While I found that Sabine Hargous' study had a rather philosophical touch, Michael Harner's study really moved me into planning myself a voyage, and it was then that I took the decision to engage on the Way of the shaman—or, to be honest, the book rather revealed me that since childhood I was on this way already, without ever knowing it, without ever being able to voice, to describe the special mission I feel is mine.

Before I got to read other of the real power stuff, so to say, because written by empirically minded researchers, and as I had to wait quite a long time to get the books from Amazon USA shipped to France, I ordered two books by Spanish authors in Barcelona, Spain, that I got within two days only and that I do not regret to have read, as they deal with the philosophical and conceptional issues.

The first was a book from the foremost Spanish authorities on the subject of shamanism, Josep M. Fericla, entitled *Al Trasluz de la Ayahuasca (2002)*. Reading this book, I realized that in Spain there is absolutely no *moralistic bias* against psychedelics such as, for example in France, and in Great Britain or the USA.

But compared to France, the legislation even in the United States is still quite liberal.

France is really the worst one can imagine in any of the Western nations, and this is after all well comprehensible when you look at the Cartesian mindset of French people, their extreme left-brainism and their almost total lack of true spirituality.

In Spain, the exact contrary is true which obviously has nothing to do with left or right-wing governments. In Spain, nobody would get the idea to put Cannabis on the index. It is as legal as Cuban cigars and perhaps more healthy than those.

The second impression was that for this Spanish author, the psychedelic quest was a real parallel way of perception, serious, not only for freaks and pioneers in consciousness exploration, but also for philosophers.

Fericla is one of the finest scholars in Spain, and not just for his preoccupation with psychedelics, but in general. Thus, a book from a real authority, and written with a serious mind and true commitment for consciousness exploration.

This book confirmed my decision to really take on the voyage I had planned and not just do a theoretical research on the topic of shamanism within the greater project of my research on the *Eight Dynamic Patterns of Living*.

The literary magazine *El Idiota* that I equally had ordered in Spain contained many interesting contributions one of which I wish to mention here as I find it very important.

This special issue of the magazine entitled *Visionarios*, contains an article about Carlos Castaneda. *Carlos Castaneda: El Enigma del Último Nagual* is a very interesting article by Cristóbal Cobo Quintas that deals with the somewhat mysterious content of Castaneda's well-known spiritual apprenticeship with the Yaqui sorcerer Don Juan.

This Spanish author sees the importance of Castaneda's books—be they invented as a part of the media debate about Castaneda pretends, be they real accounts of the practices of one of the last living witnesses of Toltec culture.

It is noteworthy that Castaneda, *inter alia* on his web site, claims to be the only legitimate last descendant of the Toltecs and spokesman for their culture within a largely ignorant world. In fact, what we learn through visions is more than just the visions; this was already clear to me when I read Castaneda myself, more than ten years ago.

And what all serious studies and reports about visionary experiences, at least those done with Ayahuasca, other DMT derivates or Peyote converge to is to affirm that these visions enhance our understanding of nature. In addition, these studies contribute to helping us understand what is *direct perception* or, as we would call it today, *systems intelligence.*

In my personal view it's not even the visions themselves that have this impact upon our intelligence but some kind of telepathic code written into the visions, but that we are not aware of, and which is transmitted directly into our DNA or, if already contained in it, thus activated or stimulated.

Eventually the books arrived from the USA and the first one I read was Ralph Metzner's excellent book about Ayahuasca—Ralph Metzner, *Ayahuasca: Human Consciousness and the Spirits of Nature (1999)*—which is actually a sampler that he edited and in which many people related personal experiences with Ayahuasca.

This book, including Metzner's highly interesting introduction, is through and through a masterpiece because it gives so many insights *simultaneously*.

It is all but a dry scientific report, but an exciting adventure to read. In a way, one cannot but feel all those individual experiences on almost a gut level, in order to definitely, and once for all, put aside a Cartesian worldview that tries to split the world off in nice little tartlets called 'science,' 'emotions,' 'perception,' 'experience,' etc.

One then begins to understand that awareness is beyond all of this while it encompasses all of this, awareness being the very fact of being aware of being aware. To begin with, it is interesting to see what the primary motivation was for most if not all of the people who contributed to the reader, most of them being involved in natural healing, or otherwise working in social professions.

These people all had in common that they expected some tangible results from the experience, for becoming better healers or advisors, or for solving personal problems, and there was none of them that did not at the end of their statements confirm that the experience had been worth it and helped them to reach this goal.

The next book I was reading, and that I found even more mind-boggling was Jeremy Narby's *The Cosmic Serpent (1999)*.

This book, written by a Swiss anthropologist, originally written in French, takes a completely different perspective. Narby, questioning the native shaman's conviction that plants really transfer knowledge during the visions, states:

> First, hallucinations cannot be the source of real information, because to consider them as such is the definition of psychosis. Western knowledge considers hallucinations to be at best illusions, at worst morbid phenomena. Second, plants do not communicate like human beings. Scientific theories of communication consider that only human beings use abstract symbols like words and pictures and that plants do not relay information in the form of mental images. For science, the human brain is the source of hallucinations, which psychoactive plants trigger by way of the hallucinogenic molecules they contain. (Id., 42)

He then puts up the hypothesis that what the plants actually do is to open a *perception channel* to our own DNA's photon vibrations.

Photon radiation of the DNA has been confirmed in recent quantum science but physicists did not go as far as saying that this photon radiation's information flow was in any way consciously *readable* for the human mind.

This hypothesis has something daring about it and Narby makes his point with quite an amount of writing skill.

However, I was again and again considering the premises he based his research upon, and in my opinion, Narby made a paramount mistake in failing to question these premises before he set out to write his book. Here is what I would advance against Narby's argumentation:

—Why should mind visions *not* be the source of real information? The fact that this contradicts modern psychiatry means nothing in terms of perception theory, a field that psychiatry has nothing to deal with and does not understand anything about.

—Why should it be important how *Western knowledge* considers hallucinations? To call them *morbid phenomena* is definitely not a scientific judgment, but a moralistic opinion and as such irrelevant for the scientific researcher.

—Who says that plants do *not* communicate like human beings? Who has the knowledge to deny this possibility? The natives do not say that plants communicate like human beings; they say that plants communicate with us using a form of telepathy that is *part of consciousness itself* and that makes that communication can be cross-species.

—Scientific theories of communication consider that plants do not relay information in the form of mental images, states Narby.

I want to see the treatise of communication where this is written!

This sentence is highly unscientific in itself in that theories of communication deal with human communication only and are generally silent about plant communication. The mere silence of this research regarding plant communication cannot logically be interpreted as a denial of the existence of such communication, in general. Here, Narby clearly committed a logical *faux-pas*.

—Finally the last sentence in Narby's hypothesis is equally suggestive, and not scientific in that it suggests namely that the human mind was seated in the brain and only in the brain, an assumption that is scientifically overthrown in the meantime.

Neuroscience and consciousness research now coincide in acknowledging that the mind or consciousness, while functioning through the physical brain, is not forcibly physically located in the brain, but certainly also in the pineal gland, the pituitary gland, and especially the luminous body or aura.

Some go beyond and suggest the mind was located probably everywhere, even in the cells of the skin of the feet, for example, but also outside of the body, as psychic research has confirmed since long.

But Narby's study certainly has high value in the present discussion, be it as a contradicting resource. One thing was namely clear to me from most of the German and American shamanism researchers and their publications: they do not question the possibility of plants being able to communicate information to the human mind in what form however this takes place! They do not, like Narby, start from a concept of *Western knowledge* but rather take a pioneering, open and experimental approach while sticking to the facts and avoiding speculation. And they all seem to take for granted that the mind and the brain have in common only that the brain functions like an interface for the mind to operate within us, and within all.

Thus, I found that Narby was, from the start of his book, much more restrictive and skeptical than, for example Michael Harner, Adam Gottlieb, Ralph Metzner or the McKenna brothers in their respective studies.

On a similar line of reasoning while from a totally different perspective is the DMT research of an American doctor, Rick Strassman, *DMT: The Spirit Molecule (2001)*.

Strassman was all but mystic-minded when he began his study with hundreds of patients to measure the experience of precisely dosed DMT injections in their veins.

The book, or how much I could stand of it, was quite boring to read and, as a result, my quotes collection is rather scarce, which is certainly not a mishap of the book itself but more of the reader. I just do not find much interest in this kind of soulless research that goes out to understand life from monkey experiments.

Okay, a similar marathon study once conducted in France by two sociologists to disproof astrology, was finally exactly confirming its functionality. But for a serious astrologer, such a study is a circus joke for the ignoramus because since thousands of years initiated individuals know about the cognitive value of astrology and they do not need monkey experiments to confirm this perennial knowledge.

I trust more a critical intelligent and initiated human such as, just to give an example, Michael Harner or Terence McKenna, who have taken DMT and who say with unshaken conviction that they received *knowledge*, real knowledge through the experience, and not just experienced a kaleidoscope of silly flash lights.

If shamanism research was so dull and insignificant as most medical doctors and skeptic anthropologists think it was, highly intelligent and trustworthy writers and researchers such as Schultes, Metzner, Harner or McKenna, would have to be called schoolboys. You and me know they were and are not, and that in shamanic voyages we are *not* dealing with kaleidoscopic games.

I was glad, then, to read something from a different mind, and frame of mind. Aldous Huxley, the author of the novel *Brave New World* and other great fiction and non-fiction writings, was one of the foremost witnesses in experiments with perception, altered perception and immediate perception. His book *The Doors of Perception (1954/1994)* is an enlightening account of someone who approached the psychedelic experience at first rather as a philosophical curiosity.

Huxley had no or very few preconceptions and his mindset was the one that Zen calls *the beginner's mind*; thus the ideal explorer of an unknown world, at least to our Western mindset.

And Huxley's experience was entirely positive. Reading his account, you are thrilled and charmed and at one point or the other seduced to try it yourself.

Huxley is very outspoken about the *philosophical implications* of his experience and he values it positively, so positively that he is quoted in every book published on entheogens; he figures almost like an authority while, reading him, one does not have this impression at all. His style is artful, witty and charming, more than in some of his other books, in my opinion.

The book is written from the heart, and there remains no doubt that Huxley loved this mushroom and its hallucinatory compound: *mescaline*. I think it is not a bad idea, for anybody interested in altered consciousness, to read this book as a kind of introduction.

BIBLIOGRAPHY

✳

ABRAMS, JEREMIAH (ED.)

Reclaiming the Inner Child
NEW YORK: TARCHER/PUTNAM, 1990

BACHELARD, GASTON

The Poetics of Reverie
TRANSLATED BY DANIEL RUSSELL
BOSTON: BEACON PRESS, 1971

BALTER, MICHAEL

The Goddess and the Bull
CATALHOYUK, AN ARCHAEOLOGICAL JOURNEY TO THE DAWN OF CIVILIZATION
NEW YORK: FREE PRESS, 2006

BATESON, GREGORY

Steps to an Ecology of Mind
CHICAGO: UNIVERSITY OF CHICAGO PRESS, 2000
ORIGINALLY PUBLISHED IN 1972

BERTALANFFY, LUDWIG VON

General Systems Theory
FOUNDATIONS, DEVELOPMENT, APPLICATIONS
NEW YORK: GEORGE BRAZILIER PUBLISHING, 1976

BOHM, DAVID

Wholeness and the Implicate Order
LONDON: ROUTLEDGE, 2002

Thought as a System
LONDON: ROUTLEDGE, 1994

Quantum Theory
LONDON: DOVER PUBLICATIONS, 1989

BORDEAUX-SZEKELY, EDMOND

Teaching of the Essenes from Enoch to the Dead
SEA SCROLLS
BEEKMAN PUBLISHING, 1992

Gospel of the Essenes
THE UNKNOWN BOOKS OF THE ESSENES
& LOST SCROLLS OF THE ESSENE BROTHERHOOD
BEEKMAN PUBLISHING, 1988

Gospel of Peace of Jesus Christ
BEEKMAN PUBLISHING, 1994

Gospel of Peace, 2d Vol.
I B S INTERNATIONAL PUBLISHERS

BIBLIOGRAPHY

BRENNAN, BARBARA ANN

Hands of Healing
A GUIDE TO HEALING THROUGH THE HUMAN ENERGY FIELD
NEW YORK: BANTAM, 1988

CAMPBELL, JOSEPH

The Hero With A Thousand Faces
PRINCETON: PRINCETON UNIVERSITY PRESS, 1973
(BOLLINGEN SERIES XVII)
LONDON: ORION BOOKS, 1999

Occidental Mythology
PRINCETON: PRINCETON UNIVERSITY PRESS, 1973
(BOLLINGEN SERIES XVII)
NEW YORK: PENGUIN ARKANA, 1991

The Masks of God
ORIENTAL MYTHOLOGY
NEW YORK: PENGUIN ARKANA, 1992
ORIGINALLY PUBLISHED 1962

The Power of Myth
WITH BILL MOYERS
ED. BY SUE FLOWERS
NEW YORK: ANCHOR BOOKS, 1988

CAPRA, BERNT AMADEUS

Mindwalk
A FILM FOR PASSIONATE THINKERS
BASED UPON FRITJOF CAPRA'S THE TURNING POINT
NEW YORK: TRITON PICTURES, 1990

CAPRA, FRITJOF

The Turning Point
SCIENCE, SOCIETY AND THE RISING CULTURE
NEW YORK: SIMON & SCHUSTER, 1987
ORIGINAL AUTHOR COPYRIGHT, 1982

The Tao of Physics
AN EXPLORATION OF THE PARALLELS BETWEEN MODERN
PHYSICS AND EASTERN MYSTICISM
NEW YORK: SHAMBHALA PUBLICATIONS, 2000
(NEW EDITION) ORIGINALLY PUBLISHED IN 1975

The Web of Life
A NEW SCIENTIFIC UNDERSTANDING OF LIVING SYSTEMS
NEW YORK: DOUBLEDAY, 1997
AUTHOR COPYRIGHT 1996

The Hidden Connections
INTEGRATING THE BIOLOGICAL, COGNITIVE AND SOCIAL
DIMENSIONS OF LIFE INTO A SCIENCE OF SUSTAINABILITY
NEW YORK: DOUBLEDAY, 2002

Steering Business Toward Sustainability
NEW YORK: UNITED NATIONS UNIVERSITY PRESS, 1995

Uncommon Wisdom
CONVERSATIONS WITH REMARKABLE PEOPLE
NEW YORK: BANTAM, 1989

The Science of Leonardo
INSIDE THE MIND OF THE GREAT GENIUS OF THE RENAISSANCE
NEW YORK: ANCHOR BOOKS, 2008
NEW YORK: BANTAM DOUBLEDAY, 2007 (FIRST PUBLISHING)

BIBLIOGRAPHY

CASTANEDA, CARLOS

The Teachings of Don Juan
A YAQUI WAY OF KNOWLEDGE
WASHINGTON: SQUARE PRESS, 1985

Journey to Ixtlan
WASHINGTON: SQUARE PRESS: 1991

Tales of Power
WASHINGTON: SQUARE PRESS, 1991

The Second Ring of Power
WASHINGTON: SQUARE PRESS, 1991

DAVID-NEEL, ALEXANDRA

Magic and Mystery in Tibet
NEW YORK: DOVER PUBLICATIONS, 1971

The Secret Oral Teachings in Tibetan Buddhist Sects
NEW YORK: SECRETS OF LIGHT PUBLISHERS, 1981

Initiations and Initiates in Tibet
NEW YORK: DOVER PUBLICATIONS, 1993

Immortality and Reincarnation
WISDOM FROM THE FORBIDDEN JOURNEY
NEW YORK: INNER TRADITION, 1997

DAVIDSON, GUSTAV

A Dictionary of Angels
INCLUDING FALLEN ANGELS
NEW YORK: FREE PRESS, 1967

DELACOUR, JEAN-BAPTISTE

Glimpses of the Beyond
NEW YORK: BANTAM DELL, 1975

DiCARLO, RUSSELL E. (ED.)

Towards A New World View
CONVERSATIONS AT THE LEADING EDGE
ERIE, PA: EPIC PUBLISHING, 1996

DÜRCKHEIM, KARLFRIED GRAF

Hara: The Vital Center of Man
ROCHESTER: INNER TRADITIONS, 2004

Zen and Us
NEW YORK: PENGUIN ARKANA 1991

The Call for the Master
NEW YORK: PENGUIN BOOKS, 1993

Absolute Living
THE OTHERWORLDLY IN THE WORLD AND THE PATH TO MATURITY
NEW YORK: PENGUIN ARKANA, 1992

The Way of Transformation
DAILY LIFE AS A SPIRITUAL EXERCISE
LONDON: ALLEN & UNWIN, 1988

The Japanese Cult of Tranquility
LONDON: RIDER, 1960

EDEN, DONNA & FEINSTEIN, DAVID

Energy Medicine
NEW YORK: TARCHER/PUTNAM, 1998

BIBLIOGRAPHY

The Energy Medicine Kit
SIMPLE EFFECTIVE TECHNIQUES TO HELP YOU BOOST YOUR VITALITY
BOULDER, CO.: SOUNDS TRUE EDITIONS, 2004

The Promise of Energy Psychology
WITH DAVID FEINSTEIN AND GARY CRAIG
REVOLUTIONARY TOOLS FOR DRAMATIC PERSONAL CHANGE
NEW YORK: JEREMY P. TARCHER/PENGUIN, 2005

EISLER, RIANE

The Chalice and the Blade
OUR HISTORY, OUR FUTURE
SAN FRANCISCO: HARPER & ROW, 1995

Sacred Pleasure: Sex, Myth and the Politics of the Body
NEW PATHS TO POWER AND LOVE
SAN FRANCISCO: HARPER & ROW, 1996

The Partnership Way
NEW TOOLS FOR LIVING AND LEARNING
WITH DAVID LOYE
BRANDON, VT: HOLISTIC EDUCATION PRESS, 1998

The Real Wealth of Nations
CREATING A CARING ECONOMICS
SAN FRANCISCO: BERRETT-KOEHLER PUBLISHERS, 2008

ELIADE, MIRCEA

Shamanism
ARCHAIC TECHNIQUES OF ECSTASY
NEW YORK: PANTHEON BOOKS, 1964

ELWIN, V.

The Muria and their Ghotul
BOMBAY: OXFORD UNIVERSITY PRESS, 1947

ERICKSON, MILTON H.

My Voice Will Go With You
THE TEACHING TALES OF MILTON H. ERICKSON
BY SIDNEY ROSEN (ED.)
NEW YORK: NORTON & CO., 1991

Complete Works 1.0, CD-ROM
NEW YORK: MILTON H. ERICKSON FOUNDATION, 2001

ERIKSON, ERIK H.

Childhood and Society
NEW YORK: NORTON, 1993
FIRST PUBLISHED IN 1950

EVANS-WENTZ, WALTER YEELING

The Fairy Faith in Celtic Countries
LONDON: FROWDE, 1911
REPUBLISHED BY DOVER PUBLICATIONS
(MINNEOLA, NEW YORK), 2002

FERICLA, JOSEP M.

Al trasluz de la Ayahuasca
ANTROPOLOGÍA COGNITIVA, ONIROMANCIA Y CONSCIENCIAS ALTERNATIVAS
BARCELONA: LA LIEBRE DE MARZO, 2002

FORTE, ROBERT (ED.)

Entheogens and the Future of Religion
COUNCIL ON SPIRITUAL PRACTICES, 2ND ED., 2000

BIBLIOGRAPHY

FOXWOOD, ORION

The Faery Teachings
ARCATA, CA: R.J. STEWARD BOOKS, 2007

FREUD, SIGMUND

Totem and Taboo
NEW YORK: ROUTLEDGE, 1999
ORIGINALLY PUBLISHED IN 1913

FROMM, ERICH

The Anatomy of Human Destructiveness
NEW YORK: OWL BOOK, 1992 (ORIGINALLY PUBLISHED IN 1973)

Escape from Freedom
NEW YORK: OWL BOOKS, 1994
ORIGINALLY PUBLISHED IN 1941

To Have or To Be
NEW YORK: CONTINUUM INTERNATIONAL PUBLISHING, 1996
ORIGINALLY PUBLISHED IN 1976

The Art of Loving
NEW YORK: HARPERPERENNIAL, 2000
ORIGINALLY PUBLISHED IN 1956

GERBER, RICHARD

A Practical Guide to Vibrational Medicine
ENERGY HEALING AND SPIRITUAL TRANSFORMATION
NEW YORK: HARPER & COLLINS, 2001

GELLER, URI

The Mindpower Kit
INCLUDES BOOK, AUDIOTAPE, QUARTZ CRYSTAL AND MEDITATION CIRCLE
NEW YORK: PENGUIN, 1996

GIMBUTAS, MARIJA

The Language of the Goddess
LONDON: THAMES & HUDSON, 2001

GORDON WASSON, R.

The Road to Eleusis
UNVEILING THE SECRET OF THE MYSTERIES
WITH ALBERT HOFMANN, HUSTON SMITH, CARL RUCK AND PETER WEBSTER
BERKELEY, CA: NORTH ATLANTIC BOOKS, 2008

GOSWAMI, AMIT

The Self-Aware Universe
HOW CONSCIOUSNESS CREATES THE MATERIAL WORLD
NEW YORK: TARCHER/PUTNAM, 1995

GOTTLIEB, ADAM

Peyote and Other Psychoactive Cacti
RONIN PUBLISHING, 2ND EDITION, 1997

GREENE, LIZ

The Mythic Journey
WITH JULIET SHARMAN-BURKE
THE MEANING OF MYTH AS A GUIDE FOR LIFE
NEW YORK: SIMON & SCHUSTER (FIRESIDE), 2000

BIBLIOGRAPHY

The Mythic Tarot
WITH JULIET SHARMAN-BURKE
NEW YORK: SIMON & SCHUSTER (FIRESIDE), 2001
ORIGINALLY PUBLISHED IN 1986

GREER, JOHN MICHAEL

Earth Divination, Earth Magic
A PRACTICAL GUIDE TO GEOMANCY
NEW YORK: LLEWELLYN PUBLICATIONS, 1999

GRINSPOON, LESTER

Marihuana
THE FORBIDDEN MEDICINE
WITH JAMES B. BAKALAR
NEW HAVEN, CT: YALE UNIVERSITY PRESS, 1997
FIRST PUBLISHED IN 1971

GROF, STANISLAV

Ancient Wisdom and Modern Science
NEW YORK: STATE UNIVERSITY OF NEW YORK PRESS, 1984

Beyond the Brain
BIRTH, DEATH AND TRANSCENDENCE IN PSYCHOTHERAPY
NEW YORK: STATE UNIVERSITY OF NEW YORK, 1985

LSD: Doorway to the Numinous
THE GROUNDBREAKING PSYCHEDELIC RESEARCH INTO REALMS OF THE
HUMAN UNCONSCIOUS
ROCHESTER: PARK STREET PRESS, 2009

Realms of the Human Unconscious
OBSERVATIONS FROM LSD RESEARCH
NEW YORK: E.P. DUTTON, 1976

The Cosmic Game
EXPLORATIONS OF THE FRONTIERS OF HUMAN CONSCIOUSNESS
NEW YORK: STATE UNIVERSITY OF NEW YORK PRESS, 1998

The Holotropic Mind
THE THREE LEVELS OF HUMAN CONSCIOUSNESS
WITH HAL ZINA BENNETT
NEW YORK: HARPERCOLLINS, 1993

When the Impossible Happens
ADVENTURES IN NON-ORDINARY REALITY
LOUISVILLE, CO: SOUNDS TRUE, 2005

GURDJIEFF, GEORGE IVANOVICH

The Herald of Coming Good
LONDON: SAMUEL WEISER, 1933

HALL, MANLY P.

The Pineal Gland
THE EYE OF GOD
EXTRACTED FROM THE BOOK: MAN THE GRAND SYMBOL OF THE MYSTERIES
KESSINGER PUBLISHING REPRINT

The Secret Teachings of All Ages
READER'S EDITION
NEW YORK: TARCHER/PENGUIN, 2003
ORIGINALLY PUBLISHED IN 1928

HAMEROFF, NEWBERG, WOOLF, BIERMAN ET AL.

Consciousness
20 SCIENTISTS INTERVIEWED
DIRECTOR: GREGORY ALSBURY
5 DVD BOX SET, 540 MIN.
NEW YORK: ALSBURY FILMS, 2003

BIBLIOGRAPHY

HARGOUS, SABINE

Les appeleurs d'âmes
L'UNIVERS CHAMANIQUE DES INDIENS DES ANDES
PARIS: ALBIN MICHEL, 1985

HARNER, MICHAEL

Ways of the Shaman
NEW YORK: BANTAM, 1982
ORIGINALLY PUBLISHED IN 1980

HERMES TRISMEGISTOS

Corpus Hermeticum
NEW YORK: EDAF, 2001

HICKS, ESTHER AND JERRY

The Amazing Power of Deliberate Intent
LIVING THE ART OF ALLOWING
CARLSBAD, CA: HAY HOUSE, 2006

HOFMANN, ALBERT

LSD, My Problem Child
REFLECTIONS ON SACRED DRUGS, MYSTICISM AND SCIENCE
SANTA CRUZ, CA: MULTIDISCIPLINARY ASSOCIATION FOR PSYCHEDELIC STUDIES,
2009
ORIGINALLY PUBLISHED IN 1980

HOLMES, ERNST

The Science of Mind
A PHILOSOPHY, A FAITH, A WAY OF LIFE
NEW YORK: JEREMY P. TARCHER/PUTNAM, 1998
FIRST PUBLISHED IN 1938

HOUSTON, JEAN

The Possible Human
A COURSE IN ENHANCING YOUR PHYSICAL, MENTAL, AND CREATIVE ABILITIES
NEW YORK: JEREMY P. TARCHER/PUTNAM, 1982

HUANG, ALFRED

The Complete I Ching
THE DEFINITE TRANSLATION FROM TAOIST MASTER ALFRED HUANG
ROCHESTER, NY: INNER TRADITIONS, 1998

HUNT, VALERIE

Infinite Mind
SCIENCE OF THE HUMAN VIBRATIONS OF CONSCIOUSNESS
MALIBU, CA: MALIBU PUBLISHING, 2000

HUXLEY, ALDOUS

The Doors of Perception and Heaven and Hell
LONDON: HARPERCOLLINS (FLAMINGO), 1994
(ORIGINALLY PUBLISHED IN 1954)

The Perennial Philosophy
SAN FRANCISCO: HARPER & ROW, 1970

JACKSON, NIGEL

The Rune Mysteries
WITH SILVER RAVENWOLF
ST. PAUL, MINN.: LLEWELLYN PUBLICATIONS, 2000
NEW YORK: ABRADALE PRESS, 1996

BIBLIOGRAPHY

JANOV, ARTHUR

Primal Man
THE NEW CONSCIOUSNESS
NEW YORK: CROWELL, 1975

JUNG, CARL GUSTAV

Archetypes of the Collective Unconscious
IN: THE BASIC WRITINGS OF C.G. JUNG
NEW YORK: THE MODERN LIBRARY, 1959, 358-407

Collected Works
NEW YORK, 1959

On the Nature of the Psyche
IN: THE BASIC WRITINGS OF C.G. JUNG
NEW YORK: THE MODERN LIBRARY, 1959, 47-133

Psychological Types
COLLECTED WRITINGS, VOL. 6
PRINCETON: PRINCETON UNIVERSITY PRESS, 1971

Psychology and Religion
IN: THE BASIC WRITINGS OF C.G. JUNG
NEW YORK: THE MODERN LIBRARY, 1959, 582-655

Religious and Psychological Problems of Alchemy
IN: THE BASIC WRITINGS OF C.G. JUNG
NEW YORK: THE MODERN LIBRARY, 1959, 537-581

The Basic Writings of C.G. Jung
NEW YORK: THE MODERN LIBRARY, 1959

The Development of Personality
COLLECTED WRITINGS, VOL. 17
PRINCETON: PRINCETON UNIVERSITY PRESS, 1954

The Meaning and Significance of Dreams
BOSTON: SIGO PRESS, 1991

The Myth of the Divine Child
IN: ESSAYS ON A SCIENCE OF MYTHOLOGY
PRINCETON, N.J.: PRINCETON UNIVERSITY PRESS BOLLINGEN
SERIES XXII, 1969. (WITH KARL KERENYI)

Two Essays on Analytical Psychology
COLLECTED WRITINGS, VOL. 7
PRINCETON: PRINCETON UNIVERSITY PRESS, 1972
FIRST PUBLISHED BY ROUTLEDGE & KEGAN PAUL, LTD., 1953

KALWEIT, HOLGER

Shamans, Healers and Medicine Men
BOSTON AND LONDON: SHAMBHALA, 1992
ORIGINALLY PUBLISHED WITH KÖSEL VERLAG, MUNICH, IN 1987

KARAGULLA, SHAFICA

The Chakras
CORRELATIONS BETWEEN MEDICAL SCIENCE AND CLAIRVOYANT OBSERVATION
WITH DORA VAN GELDER KUNZ
WHEATON: QUEST BOOKS, 1989

KIANG, KOK KOK

The I Ching
AN ILLUSTRATED GUIDE TO THE CHINESE ART OF DIVINATION
SINGAPORE: ASIAPAC, 1993

KINGSTON, KAREN

Creating Sacred Space With Feng Shui
NEW YORK: BROADWAY BOOKS, 1997

BIBLIOGRAPHY

KLIMO, JON

Channeling
INVESTIGATIONS ON RECEIVING INFORMATION FROM PARANORMAL SOURCES
NEW YORK: NORTH ATLANTIC BOOKS, 1988

KOESTLER, ARTHUR

The Act of Creation
NEW YORK: PENGUIN ARKANA, 1989.
ORIGINALLY PUBLISHED IN 1964

KRISHNAMURTI, J.

Freedom From The Known
SAN FRANCISCO: HARPER & ROW, 1969

The First and Last Freedom
SAN FRANCISCO: HARPER & ROW, 1975

Education and the Significance of Life
LONDON: VICTOR GOLLANCZ, 1978

Commentaries on Living
FIRST SERIES
LONDON: VICTOR GOLLANCZ, 1985

Commentaries on Living
SECOND SERIES
LONDON: VICTOR GOLLANCZ, 1986

Krishnamurti's Journal
LONDON: VICTOR GOLLANCZ, 1987

Krishnamurti's Notebook
LONDON: VICTOR GOLLANCZ, 1986

Beyond Violence
LONDON: VICTOR GOLLANCZ, 1985

Beginnings of Learning
NEW YORK: PENGUIN, 1986

The Penguin Krishnamurti Reader
NEW YORK: PENGUIN, 1987

On God
SAN FRANCISCO: HARPER & ROW, 1992

On Fear
SAN FRANCISCO: HARPER & ROW, 1995

The Essential Krishnamurti
SAN FRANCISCO: HARPER & ROW, 1996

The Ending of Time
WITH DR. DAVID BOHM
SAN FRANCISCO: HARPER & ROW, 1985

LABATE, BEATRIZ CALUBY

Ayahuasca Religions
A COMPREHENSIVE BIBLIOGRAPHY AND CRITICAL ESSAYS
SANTA CRUZ, CA: MAPS, 2009

LAING, RONALD DAVID

Divided Self
NEW YORK: VIKING PRESS, 1991

R.D. Laing and the Paths of Anti-Psychiatry
ED., BY Z. KOTOWICZ
LONDON: ROUTLEDGE, 1997

The Politics of Experience
NEW YORK: PANTHEON, 1983

BIBLIOGRAPHY

LAKHOVSKY, GEORGES

Secret of Life
NEW YORK: KESSINGER PUBLISHING, 2003

LASZLO, ERVIN

Science and the Akashic Field
AN INTEGRAL THEORY OF EVERYTHING
ROCHESTER: INNER TRADITIONS, 2004

Quantum Shift to the Global Brain
HOW THE NEW SCIENTIFIC REALITY CAN CHANGE US AND OUR WORLD
ROCHESTER: INNER TRADITIONS, 2008

Science and the Reenchantment of the Cosmos
THE RISE OF THE INTEGRAL VISION OF REALITY
ROCHESTER: INNER TRADITIONS, 2006

The Akashic Experience
SCIENCE AND THE COSMIC MEMORY FIELD
ROCHESTER: INNER TRADITIONS, 2009

The Chaos Point
THE WORLD AT THE CROSSROADS
NEWBURYPORT, MA: HAMPTON ROADS PUBLISHING, 2006

LEADBEATER, CHARLES WEBSTER

Astral Plane
ITS SCENERY, INHABITANTS AND PHENOMENA
KESSINGER PUBLISHING REPRINT EDITION, 1997

Dreams
WHAT THEY ARE AND HOW THEY ARE CAUSED
LONDON: THEOSOPHICAL PUBLISHING SOCIETY, 1903
KESSINGER PUBLISHING REPRINT EDITION, 1998

The Inner Life
CHICAGO: THE RAJPUT PRESS, 1911

LEARY, TIMOTHY

Our Brain is God
BERKELEY, CA: RONIN PUBLISHING, 2001
AUTHOR COPYRIGHT 1988

LEBOYER, FREDERICK

Birth Without Violence
NEW YORK, 1975

Inner Beauty, Inner Light
NEW YORK: NEWMARKET PRESS, 1997

Loving Hands
THE TRADITIONAL ART OF BABY MASSAGE
NEW YORK: NEWMARKET PRESS, 1977

The Art of Breathing
NEW YORK: NEWMARKET PRESS, 1991

LENIHAN, EDDIE

Meeting the Other Crowd
THE FAIRY STORIES OF HIDDEN IRELAND
WITH CAROLYN EVE GREEN
NEW YORK: JEREMY P. TARCHER/PENGUIN, 2004
AUTHORS COPYRIGHT 2003

LEONARD, GEORGE, MURPHY, MICHAEL

The Live We Are Given
A LONG TERM PROGRAM FOR REALIZING THE
POTENTIAL OF BODY, MIND, HEART AND SOUL
NEW YORK: JEREMY P. TARCHER/PUTNAM, 1984

BIBLIOGRAPHY

LIEDLOFF, JEAN

Continuum Concept
IN SEARCH OF HAPPINESS LOST
NEW YORK: PERSEUS BOOKS, 1986
FIRST PUBLISHED IN 1977

LIPTON, BRUCE

The Biology of Belief
UNLEASHING THE POWER OF CONSCIOUSNESS, MATTER AND MIRACLES
SANTA ROSA, CA: MOUNTAIN OF LOVE/ELITE BOOKS, 2005

LONG, MAX FREEDOM

The Secret Science at Work
THE HUNA METHOD AS A WAY OF LIFE
MARINA DEL REY: DE VORSS PUBLICATIONS, 1995
ORIGINALLY PUBLISHED IN 1953

Growing Into Light
A PERSONAL GUIDE TO PRACTICING THE HUNA METHOD,
MARINA DEL REY: DE VORSS PUBLICATIONS, 1955

LOWEN, ALEXANDER

Fear of Life
NEW YORK: BIOENERGETIC PRESS, 2003

Honoring the Body
THE AUTOBIOGRAPHY OF ALEXANDER LOWEN
NEW YORK: BIOENERGETIC PRESS, 2004

Joy
THE SURRENDER TO THE BODY AND TO LIFE
NEW YORK: PENGUIN, 1995

Narcissism: Denial of the True Self
NEW YORK: MACMILLAN, COLLIER BOOKS, 1983

Pleasure: A Creative Approach to Life
NEW YORK: BIOENERGETICS PRESS, 2004
FIRST PUBLISHED IN 1970

The Language of the Body
PHYSICAL DYNAMICS OF CHARACTER STRUCTURE
NEW YORK: BIOENERGETICS PRESS, 2006

LUNA, LUIS EDUARDO & AMARINGO, PABLO

Ayahuasca Visions
NORTH ATLANTIC BOOKS, 1999

LUTYENS, MARY

Krishnamurti: The Years of Fulfillment
NEW YORK: AVON BOOKS, 1983

The Life and Death of Krishnamurti
CHENNAI: KRISHNAMURTI FOUNDATION INDIA, 1990

LUTZBETAK, LOUIS J.

Marriage and the Family in Caucasia
VIENNA, 1951, FIRST REPRINTING, 1966

MACK, CAROL K. & MACK, DINAH

A Field Guide to Demons, Fairies, Fallen Angels, and Other Subversive Spirits
NEW YORK: OWL BOOKS, 1998

MAHARSHI, RAMANA

The Collected Works of Ramana Maharshi
NEW YORK: SRI RAMANASRAMAM, 2002

BIBLIOGRAPHY

The Essential Teachings of Ramana Maharshi
A VISUAL JOURNEY
NEW YORK: INNER DIRECTIONS PUBLISHING, 2002
BY MATTHEW GREENBLAD

MALACHI, TAU

Gnosis of the Cosmic Christ
A GNOSTIC CHRISTIAN KABBALAH
ST. PAUL: LLEWELLYN PUBLICATIONS, 2005

MALINOWSKI, BRONISLAW

Crime und Custom in Savage Society
LONDON: KEGAN, 1926

Sex and Repression in Savage Society
LONDON: KEGAN, 1927

The Sexual Life of Savages in North West Melanesia
NEW YORK: HALYCON HOUSE, 1929

MARCINIAK, BARBARA

Bringers of the Dawn
TEACHINGS FROM THE PLEIADIANS
NEW YORK: BEAR & CO., 1992

McCAREY, WILLIAM A.

In Search of Healing
WHOLE-BODY HEALING THROUGH THE MIND-BODY-SPIRIT CONNECTION
NEW YORK: BERKLEY PUBLISHING, 1996

MCKENNA, TERENCE

The Archaic Revival
SAN FRANCISCO: HARPER & ROW, 1992

Food of The Gods
A RADICAL HISTORY OF PLANTS, DRUGS AND HUMAN EVOLUTION
LONDON: RIDER, 1992

The Invisible Landscape
MIND HALLUCINOGENS AND THE I CHING
NEW YORK: HARPERCOLLINS, 1993
(WITH DENNIS MCKENNA)

True Hallucinations
BEING THE ACCOUNT OF THE AUTHOR'S EXTRAORDINARY
ADVENTURES IN THE DEVIL'S PARADISE
NEW YORK: FINE COMMUNICATIONS, 1998

MCNIFF, SHAUN

Art as Medicine
BOSTON: SHAMBHALA, 1992

Art as Therapy
CREATING A THERAPY OF THE IMAGINATION
BOSTON/LONDON: SHAMBHALA, 1992

Trust the Process
AN ARTIST'S GUIDE TO LETTING GO
NEW YORK: SHAMBHALA PUBLICATIONS, 1998

MCTAGGART, LYNNE

The Field
THE QUEST FOR THE SECRET FORCE OF THE UNIVERSE
NEW YORK: HARPER & COLLINS, 2002

BIBLIOGRAPHY

MEAD, MARGARET

Sex and Temperament in Three Primitive Societies
NEW YORK, 1935

MEADOWS, DONELLA H.

Thinking in Systems
A PRIMER
WHITE RIVER, VT: CHELSEA GREEN PUBLISHING, 2008

MEHTA, ROHIT

J. Krishnamurti and the Nameless Experience
A COMPREHENSIVE DISCUSSION OF J. KRISHNAMURTI'S APPROACH TO LIFE
DELHI: MOTILAL BANARSIDASS PUBLISHERS, 2002

MERLEAU-PONTY, MAURICE

Phenomenology of Perception
LONDON: ROUTLEDGE, 1995
ORIGINALLY PUBLISHED 1945

METZNER, RALPH (ED.)

Ayahuasca, Human Consciousness and the Spirits of Nature
ED. BY RALPH METZNER, PH.D
NEW YORK: THUNDER'S MOUTH PRESS, 1999

The Psychedelic Experience
A MANUAL BASED ON THE TIBETAN BOOK OF THE DEAD
WITH TIMOTHY LEARY AND RICHARD ALPERT
NEW YORK: CITADEL, 1995

MILLER, MARY & TAUBE, KARL

An Illustrated Dictionary of the Gods and Symbols of Ancient Mexico and the Maya
LONDON: THAMES & HUDSON, 1993

MONROE, ROBERT

Ultimate Journey
NEW YORK: BROADWAY BOOKS, 1994

MONTER, E. WILLIAM

Witchcraft in France and Switzerland
ITHACA & LONDON: CORNELL UNIVERSITY PRESS, 1976

MOODY, RAYMOND

The Light Beyond
NEW YORK: MASS MARKET PAPERBACK (BANTAM), 1989

MOORE, THOMAS

Care of the Soul
A GUIDE FOR CULTIVATING DEPTH AND SACREDNESS IN EVERYDAY LIFE
NEW YORK: HARPER & COLLINS, 1994

MURPHY, MICHAEL

The Future of the Body
EXPLORATIONS INTO THE FURTHER EVOLUTION OF HUMAN NATURE
NEW YORK: JEREMY P. TARCHER/PUTNAM, 1992

BIBLIOGRAPHY

MYSS, CAROLINE

The Creation of Health
THE EMOTIONAL, PSYCHOLOGICAL, AND SPIRITUAL RESPONSES THAT PROMOTE
HEALTH AND HEALING
NEW YORK: THREE RIVERS PRESS, 1998

NAPARSTEK, BELLERUTH

Your Sixth Sense
UNLOCKING THE POWER OF YOUR INTUITION
LONDON: HARPERCOLLINS, 1998

Staying Well With Guided Imagery
NEW YORK: WARNER BOOKS, 1995

NARBY, JEREMY

The Cosmic Serpent
DNA AND THE ORIGINS OF KNOWLEDGE
NEW YORK: J. P. TARCHER, 1999

NAU, ERIKA

Self-Awareness Through Huna
VIRGINIA BEACH: DONNING, 1981

NEUMANN, ERICH

The Great Mother
PRINCETON: PRINCETON UNIVERSITY PRESS, 1955
(BOLLINGEN SERIES)

NEWTON, MICHAEL

Life Between Lives
HYPNOTHERAPY FOR SPIRITUAL REGRESSION
WOODBURY, MINN.: LLEWELLYN PUBLICATIONS, 2006

NI, HUA-CHING

I Ching

The Book of Changes and the Unchanging Truth
2ND EDITION
SANTA BARBARA: SEVEN STAR COMMUNICATIONS, 1999

Esoteric Tao The Ching
THE SHRINE OF THE ETERNAL BREATH OF TAO
SANTA MONICA: COLLEGE OF TAO AND TRADITIONAL
CHINESE HEALING, 1992

The Complete Works of Lao Tzu
TAO THE CHING & HUA HU CHING
TRANSLATION AND ELUCIDATION BY HUA-CHING NI
SANTA MONICA: SEVEN STAR COMMUNICATIONS, 1995

NICHOLS, SALLIE

Jung and Tarot: An Archetypal Journey
NEW YORK: RED WHEEL/WEISER, 1986

ONG, HEAN-TATT

Amazing Scientific Basis of Feng-Shui
KUALA LUMPUR: EASTERN DRAGON PRESS, 1997

PONDER, CATHERINE

The Healing Secrets of the Ages
MARINE DEL REY: DEVORSS, 1985

BIBLIOGRAPHY

Radin, Dean

The Conscious Universe
THE SCIENTIFIC TRUTH OF PSYCHIC PHENOMENA
SAN FRANCISCO: HARPER & ROW, 1997

Entangled Minds
EXTRASENSORY EXPERIENCES IN A QUANTUM REALITY
NEW YORK: PARAVIEW POCKET BOOKS, 2006

Randall, Neville

Life After Death
LONDON: ROBERT HALE, 1999

Redfield, James

The Tenth Insight
HOLDING THE VISION
NEW YORK: WARNER BOOKS, 1996

The Celestine Prophecy
NEW YORK: WARNER BOOKS, 1995

Reid, Daniel P.

The Tao of Health, Sex & Longevity
A MODERN PRACTICAL GUIDE TO THE ANCIENT WAY
NEW YORK: SIMON & SCHUSTER, 1989

Guarding the Three Treasures
THE CHINESE WAY OF HEALTH
NEW YORK: SIMON & SCHUSTER, 1993

RICHET, CHARLES

Metapsychical Phenomena
METHODS AND OBSERVATIONS
KESSINGER PUBLISHING REPRINT EDITION, 2004
ORIGINALLY PUBLISHED IN 1905

RISO, DON RICHARD & HUDSON, RUSS

The Wisdom of the Enneagram
THE COMPLETE GUIDE TO PSYCHOLOGICAL AND SPIRITUAL GROWTH
FOR THE NINE PERSONALITY TYPES
NEW YORK: BANTAM BOOKS, 1999

ROBERTS, JANE

The Nature of Personal Reality
NEW YORK: AMBER-ALLEN PUBLISHING, 1994
FIRST PUBLISHED IN 1974

The Nature of the Psyche
ITS HUMAN EXPRESSION
NEW YORK, AMBER-ALLEN PUBLISHING, 1996
FIRST PUBLISHED IN 1979

ROMAN, SANAYA

Opening to Channel
HOW TO CONNECT WITH YOUR GUIDE
NEW YORK: H.J. KRAMER, 1987

ROSEN, SYDNEY (ED.)

My Voice Will Go With You
THE TEACHING TALES OF MILTON H. ERICKSON
NEW YORK: NORTON & CO., 1991

BIBLIOGRAPHY

Ruiz, Don Miguel

The Four Agreements
A Practical Guide to Personal Freedom
San Rafael, CA: Amber Allen Publishing, 1997

The Mastery of Love
A Practical Guide to the Art of Relationship
San Rafael, CA: Amber Allen Publishing, 1999

The Voice of Knowledge
A Practical Guide to Inner Peace
With Janet Mills
San Rafael, CA: Amber Allen Publishing, 2004

SantoPietro, Nancy

Feng Shui, Harmony by Design
How to Create a Beautiful and Harmonious Home,
New York: Putnam-Berkeley, 1996

Schrenck-Notzing, Albert von

Phenomena of Materialization
A Contribution to the Investigation of Mediumistic Teleplastics
Perspectives in Psychical Research
New York: Kegan Paul, 1920

Schultes, Richard Evans, et al.

Plants of the Gods
Their Sacred, Healing, and Hallucinogenic Powers
New York: Healing Arts Press
2nd edition, 2002

SHELDRAKE, RUPERT

A New Science of Life
THE HYPOTHESIS OF MORPHIC RESONANCE
ROCHESTER: PARK STREET PRESS, 1995

SMITH, C. MICHAEL

Jung and Shamanism in Dialogue
LONDON: TRAFFORD PUBLISHING, 2007

SPILLER, JAN

ASTROLOGY FOR THE SOUL
NEW YORK: BANTAM, 1997

STEINER, RUDOLF

Theosophy
AN INTRODUCTION TO THE SPIRITUAL PROCESSES IN HUMAN LIFE
AND IN THE COSMOS
NEW YORK: ANTHROPOSOPHIC PRESS, 1994

STONE, HAL & STONE, SIDRA

Embracing Our Selves
THE VOICE DIALOGUE MANUAL
SAN RAFAEL, CA: NEW WORLD LIBRARY, 1989

STRASSMAN, RICK

DMT: The Spirit Molecule
A DOCTOR'S REVOLUTIONARY RESEARCH INTO THE BIOLOGY OF NEAR-DEATH
AND MYSTICAL EXPERIENCES
ROCHESTER: PARK STREET PRESS, 2001

BIBLIOGRAPHY

SZASZ, THOMAS

The Myth of Mental Illness
NEW YORK: HARPER & ROW, 1984

TALBOT, MICHAEL

The Holographic Universe
NEW YORK: HARPERCOLLINS, 1992

TANSLEY, DAVID V.

Chakras, Rays and Radionics
LONDON: DANIEL COMPANY LTD., 1984

TARG, RUSSELL & KATRA, JANE

Miracles of Mind
EXPLORING NONLOCAL CONSCIOUSNESS AND SPIRITUAL HEALING
NOVATO, CA: NEW WORLD LIBRARY, 1999

TARNAS, RICHARD

Cosmos and Psyche
INTIMATIONS OF A NEW WORLD VIEW
NEW YORK: PLUME, 2007

TART, CHARLES T.

Altered States of Consciousness
A BOOK OF READINGS
HOBOKEN, N.J.: WILEY & SONS, 1969

THE TIBETAN BOOK OF THE DEAD

The Great Liberation through Hearing in the Bardo
TRANSLATED WITH COMMENTARY BY FRANCESCA
FREMANTLE & CHÖGYAM TRUNGPA
BOSTON: SHAMBHALA DRAGON EDITIONS, 1975

THORSSON, EDRED

Futhark
A HANDBOOK OF RUNE MAGIC
SAN FRANCISCO: WEISER BOOKS, 1984

TILLER, WILLIAM A.

Conscious Acts of Creation
THE EMERGENCE OF A NEW PHYSICS
ASSOCIATED PRODUCERS, 2004 (DVD)

Psychoenergetic Science
NEW YORK: PAVIOR, 2007

Conscious Acts of Creation
NEW YORK: PAVIOR, 2001

TODARO-FRANCESCHI, VIDETTE

The Enigma of Energy
WHERE SCIENCE AND RELIGION CONVERGE
NEW YORK: CROSSROAD PUBLISHING, 1991
NEW YORK: BANTAM, 1984

TOO, LILLIAN

Feng Shui
KUALA LUMPUR: KONSEP BOOKS, 1994

BIBLIOGRAPHY

Van Gelder, Dora

The Real World of Fairies
A First-Person Account
Wheaton: Quest Books, 1999
First published in 1977

Villoldo, Alberto

Healing States
A Journey Into the World of Spiritual Healing and Shamanism
With Stanley Krippner
New York: Simon & Schuster (Fireside), 1987

Dance of the Four Winds
Secrets of the Inca Medicine Wheel
With Eric Jendresen
Rochester: Destiny Books, 1995

Shaman, Healer, Sage
How to Heal Yourself and Others with the Energy Medicine
of the Americas
New York: Harmony, 2000

Healing the Luminous Body
The Way of the Shaman with Dr. Alberto Villoldo
DVD, Sacred Mysteries Productions, 2004

Mending The Past And Healing The Future with Soul Retrieval
New York: Hay House, 2005

Vitebsky, Piers

The Shaman
Voyages of the Soul, Trance, Ecstasy and Healing from Siberia to the Amazon
New York: Duncan Baird Publishers, 2001
Originally published in 1995

WILD, LEON D.

The Runes Workbook
A STEP-BY-STEP GUIDE TO LEARNING THE WISDOM OF THE STAVES
SAN DIEGO: THUNDER BAY PRESS, 2004

WILHELM HELMUT

The Wilhelm Lectures on the Book of Changes
PRINCETON: PRINCETON UNIVERSITY PRESS, 1995

WILHELM, RICHARD

The I Ching or Book of Changes
WITH C. BAYNES
3RD EDITION, BOLLINGEN SERIES XIX
PRINCETON, NJ: PRINCETON UNIVERSITY PRESS, 1967

WILLIAMS, STREPHON KAPLAN

Dreams and Spiritual Growth
WITH PATRICIA H. BERNE AND LOUIS M. SAVARY
NEW YORK: PAULIST PRESS, 1984

Dream Cards
UNDERSTAND YOUR DREAMS AND ENRICH YOUR LIFE
NEW YORK: SIMON & SCHUSTER (FIRESIDE), 1991

WING, R. L.

The I Ching Workbook
GARDEN CITY, N.Y.: DOUBLEDAY, 1984

BIBLIOGRAPHY

WOLF, FRED ALAN

Taking the Quantum Leap
THE NEW PHYSICS FOR NONSCIENTISTS
NEW YORK: HARPER & ROW, 1989

Parallel Universes
NEW YORK: SIMON & SCHUSTER, 1990

The Dreaming Universe
A MIND-EXPANDING JOURNEY INTO THE REALM WHERE
PSYCHE AND PHYSICS MEET
NEW YORK: TOUCHSTONE, 1995

The Eagle's Quest
A PHYSICIST FINDS THE SCIENTIFIC TRUTH AT THE HEART OF THE
SHAMANIC WORLD
NEW YORK: TOUCHSTONE, 1997

Mind into Matter
A NEW ALCHEMY OF SCIENCE AND SPIRIT
NEW YORK: MOMENT POINT PRESS, 2000

WYDRA, NANCILEE

Feng Shui
THE BOOK OF CURES
LINCOLNWOOD: CONTEMPORARY BOOKS, 1996

YANG, JWING-MING

Qigong, The Secret of Youth
DA MO'S MUSCLE/TENDON CHANGING AND MARROW/BRAIN WASHING CLASSICS
BOSTON, MASS.: YMAA PUBLICATION CENTER, 2000

The Root of Chinese Qigong
SECRETS FOR HEALTH, LONGEVITY, & ENLIGHTENMENT
ROSLINDALE, MA: YMAA PUBLICATION CENTER, 1997

YEATS, WILLIAM BUTLER

Irish Fairy and Folk Tales
NEW YORK: MODERN LIBRARY, 2003

Mythologies
NEW YORK: SIMON & SCHUSTER, 1998
AUTHOR COPYRIGHT 1959, RENEWED 1987 BY ANNE YEATS

YWAHOO, DHYANI

Voices of Our Ancestors
CHEROKEE TEACHINGS FROM THE WISDOM FIRE
NEW YORK: SHAMBHALA, 1987

ZNAMENSKI, ANDREI A.

Shamanism
CRITICAL CONCEPTS IN SOCIOLOGY
NEW YORK: ROUTLEDGE, 2004

ZUKAV, GARY

The Dancing Wu Li Masters
AN OVERVIEW OF THE NEW PHYSICS
NEW YORK: HARPERONE, 2001

PERSONAL NOTES

www.ingramcontent.com/pod-product-compliance
Lightning Source LLC
Chambersburg PA
CBHW030444290526
45786CB00001B/440